THE JEWISH WHITE SLAVE TRADE AND THE UNTOLD STORY OF RAQUEL LIBERMAN

LATIN AMERICAN STUDIES
VOLUME 14
GARLAND REFERENCE LIBRARY OF SOCIAL SCIENCE
VOLUME 2130

LATIN AMERICAN STUDIES
DAVID WILLIAM FOSTER, *Series Editor*

THE CONTEMPORARY PRAXIS
OF THE FANTASTIC
Borges and Cortázar
by Julio Rodríguez-Luis

TROPICAL PATHS
*Essays on Modern
Brazilian Literature*
edited by Randal Johnson

THE POSTMODERN IN LATIN
AND LATINO AMERICAN
CULTURAL NARRATIVES
Collected Essays and Interviews
edited by Claudia Ferman

READERS AND LABYRINTHS
*Detective Fiction in Borges,
Bustos Domecq, and Eco*
by Jorge Hernández Martín

MAGIC REALISM
Social Context and Discourse
by María-Elena Angulo

RESISTING BOUNDARIES
The Subject of Naturalism in Brazil
by Eva Paulino Bueno

LESBIAN VOICES
FROM LATIN AMERICA
Breaking Ground
by Elena M. Martínez

THE JEWISH DIASPORA
IN LATIN AMERICA
*New Studies on History
and Literature*
edited by David Sheinin
and Lois Baer Barr

JEWISH WRITERS
OF LATIN AMERICA
A Dictionary
edited by Darrell B. Lockhart

READERS AND
WRITERS IN CUBA
*A Social History
of Print Culture,
1830s–1990s*
by Pamela Maria Smorkaloff

BORGES AND THE
POLITICS OF FORM
by José Eduardo González

VOICES OF THE SURVIVORS
*Testimony, Mourning, and Memory
in Post-Dictatorship Argentina
(1983–1995)*
by Liria Evangelista
translated by Renzo Llorente

GENDER AND IDENTITY FORMATION
IN CONTEMPORARY
MEXICAN LITERATURE
by Marina Pérez de Mendiola

(CON)FUSING SIGNS AND
POSTMODERN POSITIONS
*Spanish American Performance,
Experimental Writing, and the
Critique of Political Confusion*
by Robert Neustadt

CHICANO/LATINO HOMOEROTIC
IDENTITIES
by David William Foster

THE JEWISH WHITE SLAVE TRADE
AND THE UNTOLD STORY OF
RAQUEL LIBERMAN
by Nora Glickman

FLASH & CRASH DAYS
*Brazilian Theater in the Post-
Dictatorship Period*
by David S. George

THE JEWISH WHITE SLAVE TRADE AND THE UNTOLD STORY OF RAQUEL LIBERMAN

NORA GLICKMAN

GARLAND PUBLISHING, INC.
A MEMBER OF THE TAYLOR & FRANCIS GROUP
NEW YORK AND LONDON
2000

Published in 2000 by
Garland Publishing Inc.
A Member of the Taylor & Francis Group
19 Union Square West
New York, NY 10003

10 9 8 7 6 5 4 3 2 1

Library of Congress Cataloging-in-Publication Data
Glickman, Nora.
      The Jewish white slave trade and the untold story of Raquel Liberman /
Nora Glickman.
          p.   cm. — (Garland reference library of the humanities. Latin
American Studies ; vol. 14)
      ISBN 0–8153–3300–5 (alk. paper)
      1. Liberman, Raquel, b. 1900. 2. Jews—Argentian—Buenos Aires Biog-
raphy.   3. Jewish women—Argentina Buenos Aires—Social conditions—
20th century.   4. Jewish criminals—Argentina—Buenos Aries—History
— 20th century.   5. Women—Argentina—Buenos Aires—Social conditions—20th century.   6. Prostitution—Argentina—Buenos Aires—History—20th century. 7. Sex-oriented businesses—Argentina—Buenos Aires
—History—20th century.   8. Zwi Migdal (Organization : Argentina)—
History. I. Title. II. Series.
F3001.9.J5G55   1999
982' . 11004924' 0092—dc21   99-40506
      [B]   CIP

Printed on acid-free, 250-year-life paper
Manufactured in the United States of America

Contents

SERIES PREFACE   vii
ACKNOWLEDGMENTS   ix
INTRODUCTION   xi

CHAPTER I: The Jewish White Slave Trade   3
CHAPTER II: The White Slave Trade in Literature   17
    In Yiddish Fiction   17
    In Latin American Fiction   28
    In Cinema   41

CHAPTER III: Raquel Liberman   51
    The Historical Version   53
    The Unknown Raquel   54
    Raquel In Fiction   60

CHAPTER IV: Documentation   63
    Of Raquel Liberman   63
    Of Yaacov Ferber   82

CHAPTER V: Correspondence   91
    Letters Translated from Yiddish (between 1921 and 1923)   95
    Letters and Notes Translated from Spanish (between 1925
       and 1963)   149

CHAPTER VI: Photographs   157
    Of Raquel Liberman   159
    Of the *Zwi Migdal*   178

BIBLIOGRAPHY   185
INDEX   189

Series Preface

The monographs in Garland's Latin American Studies series deal with significant aspects of literary writing, defined broadly and including general topics, groups of works, or treatments of specific authors and movements. Titles published have been selected on the basis of the originality of scholarship and the coherency of the theoretical underpinnings of the critical discourse. Cognizant of the fact that literary study is an ongoing dialogue between multiple voices, authors in the LAS series have chosen topics and approaches that complement attempts to revise the canon of Latin American literature and that propose new agendas for their analysis. These critical works focus on interdisciplinary approaches to Latin American issues: the bridging of national and linguistic divisions, subaltern studies, feminism, queer theory, popular culture, and minority topics, and many others topics that continue to gain increasing exposure in academic and popular culture.

David William Foster

Acknowledgments

The research for this book was carried out with the support of the Research Foundation of the City University of New York. Also contributing was a grant from the National Foundation for Jewish Culture for the development of my play "A Certain Raquel", based on the Liberman case.

Most of all I am indebted to Rosalía Rosembuj, my mother, who conducted most of the interviews with the Liberman family in Buenos Aires, and who was a co-translator of the Yiddish letters included in this book. I would also like to thank Raquel Liberman's grandchildren, Raquel and Horacio, for providing me with the original documents and letters. My thanks to Myrta Shalom for helping me get in touch with the Liberman family, and for generously sharing some of her own research on the subject; to Patricia Finzi for helping to prepare the photographs for the book, and to Mrs. Anne Reif for her invaluable assistance in editing the text.

Introduction

The term "white slavery" means that white women were involuntarily forced to perform sexual commerce with men in brothels. After 1904, international agreements obliged contracting governments to create agencies that would monitor the movements of people exporting women for prostitution. Since the white slave trade is, by its nature, clandestine, up until recently, most authors who claimed to be writing serious studies on the subject had gathered insufficient information, or knew about it only by hearsay. Even those who were more concerned with first-hand documentary evidence filled in the gaps by relying on their imagination.

The research included in this book covers the vicissitudes of the *polacas* (Polish and East European women) in history and literature. It deals in particular with a group of women who were deceitfully brought into Argentina by Jewish pimps at the turn of the century. Those men were in charge of the trafficking of the *polacas*.

The complex relationship between the Eastern European immigration to Argentina and the social, economic and political changes the country was undergoing, is noteworthy. The furor that was unleashed against organized prostitution was part of a more general anger against the criminals that dominated the social and political life of the country. Jewish elements who dealt with prostitution became the ideal target for xenophobic Argentine critics, who discriminated against all immigrants. The statistics, however, show that the number of Jews involved in the prostitution business were greatly exaggerated. The largest Jewish prostitution organization was the *Zwi Migdal*, translated from the Hebrew as "great force" and also after the name of its founder, *Zwi Migdal*.

This book will focus on an individual case, that of Raquel Liberman, a woman born in Poland in 1900 who follows the path of thousands of polacas taken away from their native country in the 1920s, and is forced to practice prostitution in Argentina.

What distinguishes Raquel Liberman from the rest of the victims of the White Slave Trade is that after practicing prostitution in Buenos Aires for four years, she had the courage to denounce the illegal traffic to the local authorities. Her action contributed to putting an end to a notorious and flourishing market.

Raquel Liberman's ordeal, as she reports in her own statements to Inspector of Police Julio Alsogaray, begins in 1924 and ends in 1929, when Raquel made a formal denunciation against the *Zwi Migdal*, an organization composed of white slavers. Although her courageous action did not destroy the prostitution traffic completely, it had very effective consequences: most of the brothels in Buenos Aires were closed and hundreds of traffickers were imprisoned or had to run away.

The study conducted for this book pays special attention to the documentation that has recently come into my hands regarding Raquel Liberman. Up to the present a part of her life was totally unknown. The personal data provided here refutes all previous claims that she was forced to work as a prostitute.

Other writings containing information about Raquel Liberman do not provide any facts about her family life, since she made every effort to keep it a secret. What is known, essentially, is Liberman's judicial trial as reported to Police Commissioner Julio Alsogaray. Nothing, however, is mentioned about Raquel's early youth. The present book covers the newly released correspondence translated textually from Yiddish by Rosalía Rosembuj and myself. The exchange of letters between Raquel Liberman and her husband, Yaacov Ferber, written between 1921 and 1922, prior to her coming to Buenos Aires, serves to illuminate an important period in her life. The letters reveal a very different person from the one previously imagined, and explain in part the very difficult circumstances that Raquel her to a career in prostitution.

The photographs of Raquel and her family, taken in the course of fifteen years (1919-1934) are of such extraordinary and surprising dimension that they move us to reexamine her case.

They throw light on the dilemma of a woman faced with cruel choices in her endeavor to fulfill her responsibilities to her family. In Raquel's daring action we find her response to a traditional sense of duty, combined with a pragmatic response to the economic conditions that prevailed in South America in the nineteen thirties.

The following pages provide new data on an obscure period in the life of Raquel Liberman and clarify the information presently available on her famous case. The battle Raquel fought had immediate impact not only on her own rights, but on the rights of many others who, like herself, were exploited unjustly. For she faced her oppressors straight on, risking her life and rejecting bribery.

It is appropriate to explain, above all, the historical context in which the Liberman case unfolds; to observe how her rebellion against her correligionists and against the system that protected them took place. This way it is possible to understand why Raquel insisted on liberating herself from their yoke and on initiating a campaign against a criminal organization as powerful as the *Zwi Migdal*.

Raquel Liberman is a person who intrigues us because of her determination to lead a double life. During her most terrible years, she does the impossible to keep her family life a secret. Even in her most notorious public declarations she never says a word to the police, the lawyers, or the judges about her children or her dead husband.

Only after analyzing the material covered in the documents, the letters and the photos provided in this book, can we appreciate the complexity of Raquel Liberman's life, and understand why her accusations provoked a response that inspired historians and researchers as much as novelists, poets and dramatists. The present study compares Raquel Liberman's own censored version of her life with the historical facts, as they have now been documented.

What sets Raquel Liberman apart was an act of rebellion that could have cost her her life. Throughout the centuries, Latin American women—Sor Juana Inés de la Cruz, Juana de Ibarbourou, Gabriela Mistral, Alfonsina Storni—left a legacy of poetry in defense of women abused by men. Going over the circumstances surrounding Raquel Liberman's life and the literature that this immigrant has inspired, it is possible to observe that, although Raquel does not acquire the dimensions of a saint, of a muse, nor even those of a martyr, she does share with the other women the valor of having raised her voice, all alone, and spoken up about her condition.

THE JEWISH WHITE SLAVE TRADE AND THE UNTOLD STORY OF RAQUEL LIBERMAN

CHAPTER I

The Jewish White Slave Trade
The Zwi Migdal

Only here there are chimneys of steamers (. . .) They unload all the elements indispensable for the construction of an immense city giving birth.

Everything!

Only the most important thing is missing . . . Woman!

Albert Londres *The Road to Buenos Ayres*

During the first decades of this century there was as yet no law that prohibited public, open prostitution in Argentina. Buenos Aires and its surroundings were swarming with brothels, and the traffickers dealing in that market enjoyed multiple privileges. They had free access to the ports, could climb aboard the arriving boats, and even remove by force those girls who offered any resistance, without facing any struggle from the authorities.

In spite of the fact that the larger number of foreign-born women arrested in Buenos Aires for scandalous behavior were Spanish, French or Italian rather than Eastern European, the persistent reference to Jewish pimps and prostitutes became a sign of religious depravity. Several historians coincide in that prostitution in Argentina was not primarily a Jewish business. The French, who catered to a richer clientele, dominated the vice scene. The Jews, in turn, were followed by the Italians and the Creoles.[1]

What is remarkable is that public accusations against Jewish delinquents made by Argentine Jews did not have a parallel among other immigrant groups, as those groups did not discriminate against their "own" pimps and prostitutes. This, in fact, in Bernardo Kordon's estimation, may be regarded as a tribute, as it "testifies to the strong moral zeal that characterized Jews in Argentina and in the rest of the world."[2]

Prostitutes were extremely reluctant to testify to the authorities for fear of reprisals from their slavers. The laws protecting minors from the trade were seldom enforced. Traffickers, for their part, did everything in their power to keep their activities secret.

As early as the mid-nineteenth century Domingo F. Sarmiento and Luis Alberdi were advocating policies which encouraged a European immigration that would drastically change the prevailing conditions in Argentina. The majority of the immigrants who came to Argentina were single and married men who were leaving their families in their native countries with the hope of gathering sufficient funds to send for them soon after.

Through previously arranged contracts—such as those of the Jewish Colonization Association—Jewish families from Eastern European countries arrived at the port of Buenos Aires from where they were directed to their farms in the provinces and distributed in the Argentine Pampas. Few of them remained for any length of time in the Capital. The immigrant Jews of this group were called *rusos*, as most had been born in Russia.

The larger immigrational Jewish group began to arrive in Argentina in 1890. Most of them (over 40,000) were agricultural pioneers brought over under the sponsorship of Baron Hirsch, a Bavarian philanthropist who wished to save them from the Pogroms in Eastern Europe. Baron Hirsch created the Jewish Colonization Association (ICA), to provide them with settlements in their "golden" land of Argentina.

Although Baron Hirsch's representative warned the new immigrants about the presence of human flesh traffickers outside the gates of the port, and advised them not to let their families into the street, a few families fell into their hands. Mordechai Alpersohn, one of the pioneers who arrived in Argentina as a farmer in 1891, commented that "near the gates of the immigration house [they] met a few dozen elegantly dressed women and fat men in top hats. Through the gates the [procurers] were talking with [the immigrants'] wives and gave chocolate to the children."[3]

In spite of the efforts of the ICA, by 1910 Argentina was stained with the image of being a "contaminated land". And trafficking was identified as a principally Jewish activity, to the point of endangering the potential immigration from Europe.

Perhaps in response to the disproportion of female to male population—a high number of males in relation to a small number of females—commercial vice began to infiltrate Argentina in the late 1880s. The great imbalance also became evident in the demographic disproportion of immigrants to natives living in the country. Since 1889, however, international agreements obliged governments to create agencies to monitor the moves of people exporting women for prostitution into Argentina.

Until 1910 prostitution in Argentina was seen as a morality issue. In response to the pervading fear of dangerous lower class women who sold their sexual favors out of dire poverty, and of those who enjoyed themselves while they earned their "immoral wages," new morality laws were passed. They required that immigrants pass literacy and medical tests, that they produce a certificate proving they had been free of a criminal record for the previous ten years, and that women under twenty-two could not enter the country alone, unless they were met by a responsible person.[4]

Although xenophobic sentiments in Argentina were directed against minority groups already living there even before 1880, when the physical presence of the Jew was almost nonexistent in Argentina, certain authors expressed exaggerated fears of the dangerous influence of Jews in their country. As critic Gladys Onega points out in her book *La inmigración en la literatura Argentina: 1800-1910*, "xenophobia has served in our country . . . as a pretext for the defense of the most conservative and antisocial values and interests."[5]

Anti-immigration conservatives linked the white slave trade with the corruption and debasement of Argentinian morality. They presented a distorted picture of the Jew based on racial prejudice and the prevailing Christian myths derived from Judas and from the Wandering Jew. The early decades of this century witnessed an increase in stereotypes of wealthy bankers (The Rothchilds, the Galeanos, the Bauer and Landawers), and a surge of the publications influenced by anti-Semitic European literature, such as the *Protocols of the Elders of Zion* and Edouard Drumont's *La France Juive.*[6]

Politicians and the public openly discriminated against foreigners and legalized prostitution. They heightened their anti-white slavery campaign and attempted to abolish municipally licensed bordellos. Consequently, pimps and prostitutes were forced create their own societies and to conduct their activities surreptitiously, with the connivance of the police, in order to evade new regulations.

CRIMINAL ORGANIZATIONS:

Although to naive minds there was no difference between one criminal Jewish group and another, during the first three decades of the twentieth century, two groups of Jews lived side by side in Buenos Aires: The "pure" ones, and the *t'meyim* (Hebrew for "unclean"). The traffickers insisted on identifying themselves as Jews, and on legitimizing their religion through rites. This was a factor that disturbed the Jewish community intensely, as they feared the possible confusions that might derive from xenophobic and antisemitic actions (Mirelman, 352).[7]

The paradox consists in that at the same time as the t'meym profess with devotion a religion of high ethical principles, they do not hesitate to practice the commerce of women. A report of the beginning of this century describes their ostentatious lifestyle:

> They wear enormous diamonds, they attend the theater or the opera daily. They hold their own clubs, where the 'merchandise' is classified, auctioned and sold. They have their own secret code . . . They feel comfortable in the Jewish neighborhood knowing that many of the tailors, shop-keepers, and jewelers depend on them as clients (Mirelman, 351).

THE "CAFTEN SOCIETY":

Feeling ostracized from their community the traffickers built their own synagogue to perform the religious ceremonies of their members, and they also built their own cemetery. The Hungarian Jews from Rio de Janeiro were the first to manage a "Caften Society"—so called because their traditionally long gowns became synonymous with pimps in charge of the illegal brothels.

THE "WARSAW SOCIETY" AND THE "ZWI MIGDAL":

A notorious institution which passed off as a mutual aid provider, was the *Warsaw Society*, founded in 1906. In 1926 the Polish Ambassador objected to the use of its name and forced it to be changed, as he considered it offensive to his country. The new name the organization adopted was *Zwi Migdal* after its founding member. Although the numbers vary, it is believed that in 1929 the *Zwi Migdal* numbered 500 members, that it controlled 2000 prostitution brothels and employed 30,000 women.[8] The *Zwi Migdal* consistently found ways to break morality rules.

THE "ASHQUENAZIM SOCIETY":

This entity, also associated with the white slave trade, reached its pinnacle of wealth and influence in 1920. It was composed principally by Russian and Rumanian Jews who hid their illegal activities, ostensibly as an Israelite Society of Mutual Help.

THE "POLACAS":

As early as 1890, when Argentina began to receive large waves of immigration, a large scale commerce of white slaves began to import women from Poland and Hungary. These women, known as *polacas* were very different from other foreign prostitutes who arrived "in a constant flow from all corners of Europe to Argentina" (Goldar, 48). "Polaca" was the generic name applied to all Jewish prostitutes in Argentina. Violations of the law, widely tolerated by corrupt officials in the customs office, facilitated their illegal entry into the country, and their spreading throughout the city of Buenos Aires.

The *polacas* were deceived by Jews of good economic standing that came to their native villages to ask for their hand in marriage. Sometimes the girls were visited by suppliers who made "contracts" which were in fact stratagems to raise the hopes of the parents, whose wish was that their virgin daughters would keep their religion and marry men who would provide them with a respectable life—even if it was in such a remote place as Buenos Aires. The parents candidly accepted the false promises from the *Alfonsos* (traffickers), and gave away their adolescent daughters to their "husbands", hoping that after a few years they would join them in a land free from poverty and antisemitism.

In *Prostitution and Prejudice* Edward Bristow also describes the international ramifications of the Jewish white slave trade in Argentina—"El dorado" dream of European traffickers.[9] What the *polacas* had left in their native country was only misery and persecution. Upon arriving in Argentina, however, most *polacas* encountered new difficulties that, paradoxically, precluded for them any possibility to adapt themselves to the country. But as opposed to the rest of European women practicing prostitution, the *polacas* soon found they did not have a place to return to, so that they had no other choice but to become an integral part of their community in Buenos Aires.

In response to the total rejection of their community, the traffickers consolidated their efforts to fund their own organizations. The acclaimed Yiddish author Leib Malach—an immigrant from Poland—reports both in journalistic entries and in his fiction how persistently the prostitutes and the traffickers had insisted on attending the synagogue of the Jewish community, and on being allowed to be buried in its Jewish cemetery.[10] Upon their rejection, their vast earnings allowed them to build their own temple and burial ground without much difficulty.

In his study on this subject, Victor Mirelman writes about the celebration of the *shtile hoopes* ("silent weddings") in Buenos Aires under the auspices of the *Zwi Migdal*. These ceremonies were not preceded by a Civil marriage, as the Argentine law prescribed.[11] In this manner the women were pushed into a miserable existence. Later they would be exploited or sold in private auctions arranged by the traffickers.

The *Zwi Migdal* also acquired a cemetery where it would bury their dead—madams of brothels, ruffians, prostitutes and suicide cases—since the Jewish community rejected them from their own cemetery.

THE TRAFFICKERS, THE POLACAS AND THE YIDDISH THEATER:

The Jewish community considered the white slave traders their worst social vice. Their moralistic attitude even caused them to deny them access to the Yiddish theaters. This behavior made such an impression on the journalist Roberto Arlt, that he commented in the Buenos Aires newspaper *El Mundo* that[12]

> The *Zwi Migdal* society has been operating in Buenos Aires for a number of years. You all know that the above mentioned society is composed of white slave traders, Poles, and Jews, or Polish Jews. The Jewish community denounced it numerous times to the police. I have even been told that in a Jewish theater there was a billboard that

stated: 'White slavers are forbidden entrance here.' That is to say, everyone knew them, even the doormen.

Gerardo Bra makes a similar observation when he points out that already by 1908 the Jewish organization "Yugnt" had issued an order not to rent places to the traffickers, and that there were situations in which right in the middle of a theatrical performance the audience would expel the unwanted elements, shouting "Out with the pimps!".[13]

Nevertheless, during the nineteen twenties, the place where white slave traders became most visible, and where they found a lax atmosphere which was congenial to their operations was the Yiddish theater, "where hundreds of prostitutes patrolled the balconies nightly, in search of customers" (Weisbrot, 14)

COUNTER-SLAVERY ORGANIZATIONS:

As the good name and the moral prestige of the Jewish community demanded the obliteration of the evil element from its midst, hundreds of women and young girls were pulled away from the hands of the traffickers and placed with families who offered to help them.

THE "SOPROTIMIS":

The "Soprotimis" defended the rights of immigrant Jews in Argentina, provided them with judicial, social, financial and moral help.[14] and, most importantly, provided information concerning the Jewish community's fight against the "impure". "Soprotimis" helped many of the women who were liberated from their *chatanim* (fiancés), and demanded their return to their native homes by providing them with tickets.

THE "EZRAT NASHIM":

Due to the indifference of the official authorities towards implementing penalties against the white slavers, the "Ezrat Nashim" society, founded in Buenos Aires in 1895, was unable to operate successfully. Its members waited for the arrival of the boats in order to alert those young women arriving alone, of the dangers in store for them. Some of those women were not easily convinced, as they had been specially "called for" by their fiancés. The women of the "Ezrat Nashim" also had to convince the local authorities of the importance of their task. After they investigated the reasons for immigrating, as well as the "morality" of the woman's relatives, they could determine whether she should be allowed to join her family or not. Those women who had no family were kept under the care of "Ezrat Nashim" until they could earn their own living, while those who were found to come for the express purpose of prostitution were sent back to their native countries.

ALBERT LONDRES' DRAMATIC VOYAGE:

The most vivid accounts of the incidents that took place between 1920 and 1930 in the traffic from Europe to Argentina, are recollected by French writer Albert Londres. His *Le Chemin de Buenos Aires* (The Road to Buenos Ayres (sic) 1923) falls between the categories of documentary reporting and the novel. Londres's account should be regarded with skepticism: although it purports to be reporting factual accounts, he fills the gaps in the narrative with creative writing. Travelling as an investigator for the League of Nations, Londres followed the voyage of women who were destined for prostitution from their places of origin in Europe (Paris, Marseille, Warsaw), across the ocean to Buenos Aires. His account is valuable because he describes both the women "who do not die by it," and the men "who live by it".

Londres focuses chiefly on the non-Jewish *francesas*, or French prostitutes, who were the most highly valued group of prostitutes. In his view, the Frenchmen who operated brothels were prepared to protect the women they exploited—including drug addiction and prostitution— provided the women would share with them the profits they made. On the popular scale of values, he observes that French women are the "aristocracy"; then come the *polacas*, and finally the lowest social group, the "serfs" or *creoles*. What the customers did with them seemed to follow a pattern: "Throw over the Creole, sharpen our claws on the Pollack, and try for the Franchucha" (Londres, 241).

In his chapter on the *polacas* he remarks, ironically on those traffickers who represent themselves officially as fur merchants; "Well . . . human skins are pelts too, I suppose!" (Londres, 170). Most strikingly, Londres reports on the business terminology used by the secret gangs that recruited the Polish women. The slavers' organization was known as "the center"; the women were called "remounts" (a term normally used for animals, meaning "fresh horses"); underage girls were known as "lightweights," while those arriving in Buenos Aires without papers were known as "false weights." Londres is moralistic about this "old problem," which, in his view, began with hunger and poverty in Europe. In exposing these conditions he goes down "into the pits where society deposits what it fears or rejects; to look at what the world has condemned" (244). Londres does not have much faith in repressive measures, such as official decrees and bans against the white slave traffic, because "they simply serve to absolve from responsibility the officials who are supposed to contend with it"(Londres, 245).

Despite Londres' claim to inform the reader and to document impartially crucial details of this traffic, his portrayal of the Jewish pimp remains a caricature:

> Those dark Levites, their filthy skins making the strangest effect of light and shade, their unwashed locks corkscrewing down their left cheeks, their flat round caps topping them like a saucepan lid . . . I shuddered; I felt as though I had fallen into a nest in which great and mysterious dark birds were spreading their wings to bar my retreat (Londres, 166).

Londres gives testimony to the transport of the traffickers with their "human load" from the poorest villages of Poland, where they relied on ritual marriages and on dowries to secure new recruits, and follows them through Warsaw, Odessa and Marseilles, to their "unloading" at the River Plate. From the start he describes the sinister operation in total awe:

> As I passed through, curtains were drawn and windows shut. Groups of Jews, who were standing about in the open, dispersed. I shuddered. I felt as though I had fallen into a nest in which great mysterious dark birds were spreading their wings to bar my retreat . . . (p. 166).

> In Warsaw, Cracaw, Livoff, and the villages like the one I describe, there are old women who are paid by them all the year round to do nothing but let them know of anything good. "Such and such a house is no good: the girls are sickly. Avoid such and such a family: the father and mother mean to ask a high price. But there, and there, you will find exactly what you want, my little brother. You must be very pious to do any business with that family. I should not "marry" this girl, but there's a girl you might well take. The younger is the best, the older is lazy. There's only a grandmother in that house and she won't last long. Take the child, she's the best bargain in the district.

I've watched her for you like a peach on a wall. You need only pick
it!" (Londres, 171).

The arrival by boat of the "packages" to Buenos Aires turns out to
be even more sordid because it describes a gratuitous sadism as part of
the training of the women by the exploiters of their own faith:

> For the first few weeks, the Polacks, unlike the French, do not spoil
> them. While awaiting the great day of their first appearance, they
> keep them in some filthy garret, so that the brothel may seem like
> paradise . . . Not a Polack in Buenos Ayres but has five or six women:
> seven: eight! (Londres, 168).

Londres aims to destroy the sentimentality usually associated with
prostitution. Recognizing the tragedy of this profession, he assigns
responsibility to everyone involved: "Until recently it was maintained
that these women were exceptional cases; scenes from a romance; the
romance of a girl betrayed; an excellent story to make mothers weep;
but merely a story; the girl who is unwilling knows where to apply"
(247). Londres is probably referring here to women's institutions such
as "Ezrat Nashim" and "Ashquenazim" based in London, which
assisted prostitutes who showed interest in rehabilitating themselves.
    Londres drowned while travelling on his second voyage of return
to Buenos Aires. He was aboard the "George Philipard", a French ship
"that burnt in the Atlantic, as it was bringing a human load of three
hundred women destined to practice prostitution in this part of South
America".[15] In the prologue to the Spanish translation of Londres'
book, the critic Andrés Chinarro suggests that the fire was of suspicious
origin. The purpose of Londres' journalistic subjective research on the
polacas was to prove that the traffickers that offered ritual weddings to
assure Polish recruits, were becoming dangerously powerful in Buenos
Aires.
    One factor which cannot be left out of account was the climate of
hostility to the slavers and their women within the Jewish community
of Buenos Aires. Despite the pressure the slavers exerted, and their
economic influence, Jewish institutions rejected them as "*t'meyim*", and
forced them, indirectly, to create their own guilds. Those outcasts
whose families insisted on burying them in the Jewish cemetery of the
community, were placed alongside the suicides, and the beggars in a
corner facing the wall. The ostracism of the Jewish community made it

harder for *Zwi Migdal* leaders to conceal themselves when they were under investigation.

THE VICTORY OFCHIEF INSPECTOR JULIO ALSOGARAY AND JUDGE RODRIGUEZ OCAMPO:

In spite of all their efforts, the Jewish communal institutions could not have eliminated the white slave trade by themselves. In 1930 a major campaign against the slavers was mounted by Julio Alsogaray, deputy commissioner of police in Buenos Aires. Frustrated and impatient at his earlier unsuccessful attempts at reform, Alsogaray made a target of the *Zwi Migdal*. After hearing the testimony of Raquel Liberman, an instrumental witness to his success, Alsogaray wrote *Trilogía de la trata de blancas: Rufianes. Policía. Municipalidad* (White Slave Trade Trilogy: Traffickers. Police. Municipality; 1931), which is a detailed report, listing the names of the men and women who operated the *Zwi Migdal*.[16] In this exposé he defines his struggle as that of "a Lilliputian against Hercules" and documents how local politicians and fellow policemen had been corrupted by Jewish traffickers.

Organized prostitution had become such a national and international embarrassment for Argentina, that in December 1931 José Guerrero, then Mayor of the Capital, issued a decree abolishing municipally licensed prostitution, closing down bordellos, and organizing an anti-venereal disease campaign. As a result of the police crackdown, several hundred members of the *Zwi Migdal* were arrested and convicted, and severe sentences were imposed by the presiding judge, Manuel Rodriguez Ocampo. The Jewish community as a whole was legally exonerated of blame. Yet even after the vigorous crackdown by the police, and in spite of Alsogaray's and Judge Ocampo's sentences, many *Zwi Migdal* members were tipped off and fled to Uruguay and Brazil, which were also tightening up their immigration laws.

At a time when more than ever before European Jewry needed it to be open, Judge Ocampo himself was considering the need to regulate immigration. The Argentine Jewish community was still pessimistic, as the sensationalism of the vice raids also provoked anti-semitic press reports. The success of the community and of the legal authorities was, however, in Bristow's words, "a pyrrhic victory"[17]: In January 1931 the Court of Appeals set free all but three of the 106 defendants that Judge Ocampo had held under preventive imprisonment, since none of their women would testify.[18] Over the next few years, with fascism on the rise, a chauvinistic climate prevailed—less permissive of vice and more hostile toward criminal acts—abolishing brothels and increasing the deportation of pimps.   After Alsogaray's book became available, other derogatory publications began to appear. As these works focused on anti-semitism—an easier target in a Catholic and conservative country—native-born prostitution was ignored. Their criticism of immigrant Jews was an implicit defense of the morality of local pimps, madams and prostitutes.[19]

Another significant factor that was instrumental in putting an end to the white slave trade, was the September 30, 1930 coup d'etat that ousted General Hipólito Yrigoyen, and that brought to power a more dictatorial government. Its leader, General José F. Uriburu curtailed immigration, raised barriers against the naturalization of foreigners already living in Argentina, and drastically restricted the slavers' operations between Europe and America, forcing most of them out of Argentina.[20]

A MODERN PERSPECTIVE ON THE ISSUE OF JEWISH WHITE SLAVERY:

Much of the research conducted on prostitution during the 1930s only served to reinforce a stereotype of the white slaver and prostitute as typically Jewish. The research conducted by historian Donna Guy shows that, paradoxically, although prostitution was seen as a morality issue, and although women were condemned for selling their sexual favors, nowhere was there any mention of men's responsibility for spreading venereal disease, or of men's unacceptable behavior.[21] Furthermore, Guy notes that the Argentine campaign against Jewish anti-slavery was linked to a long-standing desire to blame social problems on foreigners, and that Jewish traffickers were an ideal target. Throughout her research Guy demonstrates that not even in the 1920s were the Jewish organizations as powerful as their detractors imagined, and that the actions the police took against traffickers and suspected pimps were, in effect, attempts to entrap the *Zwi Migdal* members, since they represented all that was wrong with Buenos Aires. In a carefully conducted survey of Argentine brothels in 1935, the "Ezrat Nashim" found that very few Jewish women were among the inmates, and that most of those discovered were over thirty five years old.[22] It appeared to be much easier, then, to blame Jews for all the ills of the country than to face the complex relation of prostitution to Argentine society, politics and economy.

Comisario Ernesto Pareja's investigation in his *Aspectos raciales de la prostitución* (Racial Aspects of Prostitution (1937) noted the influence of foreign born madams and prostitutes that had characterized prostitution in the capital city for many years.[23] He makes a distinction between European prostitutes (Catholic or Protestant) who were superior because they had entered prostitution after long periods of misery, and Jewish prostitutes who had "no moral qualms, and their desire to obtain money was frequently the source of their degradation."[24]

NOTES

1. On the different clienteles, see Albert Londres, *The Road to Buenos Ayres*. Trans. Eric Sutton, New York: Blue Ribbon Books, 1928.

2. Bernardo Kordon, *El Mundo Israelita*, Buenos Aires, December 22, 1985.

3. Mordechai Alpersohn, *Dreissig Jahren in Argentina* (Yiddish: Thirty Years in Argentina) Vol 1,(Berlin, 1923) Ch. 2.

4. Donna Guy, *Sex and Danger in Buenos Aires* Lincoln: University of Nebraska Press, 1991, p. 104.

5. Gladys Onega, *La inmigración en la literatura Argentina: 1800-1910*, Santa Fé, 1965, p. 132.

6. Edouard Drumont, *La France Juive*. Paris: Margon & Flammarion, 1885.

7. Victor Mirelman, "The Jews of Argentina (1830-1930): Assimilation and Particularism." Ph.D. Dissertation, Columbia University, 1973, p. 352.

8. Ernesto Goldar, *La "mala vida"*. Buenos Aires: Centro Editor de América Latina, 1971.

9. Edward Bristow, *Prostitution and Prejudice: The Jewish Fights Against White Slavery*, London: Oxford Press, 1982.

10. Leib Malach, *Don Domingo's Crossroads* Ed. B. Kletzin. Editorial Vilna, Poland, 1930 A chapter of this Yiddish novel was translated into English by Nora Glickman and Rosalía Rosenbug in *Argentine Jewish Fiction*, *Modern Jewish Studies*. Ed. Nora Glickman, New York: Queens College Publications, 1989 17–32. Leib Malach *Regeneración* (Ibergus) Translation from Yiddish into Spanish by Rosalía Rosenbug and Nora Glickman Buenos Aires Editorial Pardís, 1984.

11. Víctor Mirelman, *En búsqueda de una identidad*, Buenos Aires, Editorial Milá, 1988.

12. Roberto Arlt, "Que no queden aguas de borrajas," Diario "El Mundo," Buenos Aires, April 6, 1930.

13. Gerardo Bra, *La organización negra: La increíble historia de la Zwi Migdal*, Buenos Aires: Ediciones Corregidor, 1982.

14. Robert Weisbrot, *The Jews of Argentin*a Philadelphia, Jewish Publication Society, 1979.

15 *Argentiner YWO Shriftn*, Buenos Aires, 1955.

16. Albert Londres, *El camino de Buenos Aires* (Buenos Aires: Aga Taura, 1927), p. 7.

17. Julio L. Alsogaray, *Trilogía de la trata de blancas: Rufianes -policía - municipalidad*. 2d. ed. Buenos Aires: Tor, n.d.

18. Edward Bristow, *Prostitution and Prejudice* Oxford: Oxford University Press, 1982, 318.

19. Gerardo Bra , *La organización negra: La increíble historia de la Zwi Migdal*. Buenos Aires, Corregidor, 1982. ("La Mutual," 90-91.)

20. Victorio Luis Bessero, in *Los tratantes de blancas en Buenos Aires: El escándalo de la pseudo sociedad "Varsovia" o "Migdal"*. Buenos Aires, 1930, focused on the *Zwi Migdal*'s most infamous associates, particularly on the wealthy madams.

21.. Robert Weisbrot, *The Jews of Argentina* (Philadelphia Jewish Publication Society, 1979), p. 63.

22. Donna J. Guy, *Sex and Danger in Buenos Aires*. The University of Nebraska Press, 1991.

23. J.A. Report (1936) 34.

24. Ernesto M. Pareja. *La prostitución en Buenos Aires*. Buenos Aires, Tor, 1936.

CHAPTER II

The Jewish White Slave Trade in Literature

Then in the clamor of the ebullient city,
my dark life misses the absent clarity.
I must give up my bliss and mask my name,
please the beast that turns into a man
and suffer my sorrow painstakingly . . .

Clara Béter,*Verses from a* . . .

I. THE WHITE SLAVE TRADE IN YIDDISH FICTION:

Well before the theme of the Jewish white slave trade was written about
in Latin America, European Jewish authors showed their concern about
it and discussed it in their novels. The theme of Jewish prostitution was
treated by the Yiddish short story writer Scholem Aleichem, and more
extensively by Shalom Asch.

Shalom Asch: (1880–1957)

The latter's treatment of the prostitution world is both awe-inspiring
and serious. In his play *Got fun Nekome* (God of Vengeance, 1907),
Asch explores a theme that preoccupied him throughout his life: faith
pushed to its ultimate extreme, which may result in martyrdom, is both
symbolic and naturalistic[1]. *God of Vengeance* was produced in Berlin
(in German), in St. Petersburg (in Russian) and in many American,
Australian and European cities. It brought Asch worldwide fame. Yankl

Shapshovitsh, the protagonist, operates a brothel one floor below the home he shares with his wife (who had once been a madam) and his teenage daughter. Yankl has the naive belief that if he keeps a Torah scroll in his house, it will safeguard the purity of his daughter. Rivkale, however, does not marry the religious groom intended for her, but enters a lesbian relationship with one of the prostitutes at the brothel. Her father laments the vengeance of God that has punished the only pure thing he has created.

Asch's novel *Mottke Ganev* (translated as *Mottke the Vagabond* in 1916 and as *Mottke the Thief* in 1935), describes the life of an underworld character—Mottke—and realistically captures the humiliations inflicted on the poor in Warsaw.[2] As the novel progresses, Mottke becomes a selfless, romantic hero. He is an abused child, brought up in harsh poverty, who evokes a scene in which the local pimps of Warsaw and their overseas guests do their business. There the visitors talk "a sort of Spanish-Jewish dialect, mixed with Turkish phrases and expressions drawn from every conceivable European language." Asch describes the conditions under which the transactions took place:

> The words "Buenos Aires" and the "Argentine" are for those girls surrounded with the gloriole of legend. There in Buenos Aires, girls were free, made lots of money from the "blacks", then acquired a husband and they themselves became proprietresses of establishments . . . when the dealers came from Buenos Aires to replenish their stock the Old Town held a High Holiday.

Mottke moves around in the underworld of Polish misery and corruption. On the one hand he is sentimental and generous; he is devoted to his mother and aspires to win the respect of his wife. But he also embodies the vices of some pre-war Jews, condemned to a life of crime along with a need for redemption.

Argentina only comes into the picture when the victimized women, anxious to change their lifestyle, see Buenos Aires as the Grand Monde, and take pride in being sold "for export". Intent on impressing the "morenos" (dark-skinned men) of Buenos Aires, they dye their hair blond and prepare themselves to become prosperous madams of independent establishments. They have their own exotic fantasies, stimulated by what they hear from letters they receive from their friends in Latin America. These letters tell of endless riches and of the gifts and money sent to their parents and relatives. In Buenos Aires, they learn, people brush their teeth with gold brushes, and they also wrap their teeth with gold. Furthermore, their exaggerated reports lead them to wish so much to conquer the love of "princes and black sultans" in Buenos Aires, that they take the Creoles for sheiks from Arab harems.

Sholem Aleichem: (1859-1916)

Ostensibly, Sholem Aleichem's story *The Man From Buenos Aires* deals with a Jew who returns to Poland to find a wife and to bring her back to Argentina, where he resides. The protagonist presents himself as a bright and handsome man. The irony is achieved by the lack of response from the interlocutor, who remains silent till the end of the train ride. But Mottke—the man from Buenos Aires—is not who he claims to be. He protects himself by using elliptical speech: "No doubt you would like to know what kind of work I do. You'd better not ask" (132). He never reveals his occupation, but he does offer some hints as to the sinister nature of his work:

> I supply the world with merchandise; something that everyone knows and nobody speaks of. Why? Because it's a cunning world and people are too shifty. They don't like it if you tell them black is black and white is white. They would rather have you tell them that black is white and white is black. So what can you do with them? (134).

Although Mottke pretends to remove himself from the hypocrisy he condemns in others, he boasts of his honesty and his largesse towards his future wife, and assures that in Buenos Aires he "will build her a palace fit for a princess" (139). In spite of the impudent tone with which Mottke boasts of his great fortune, he does display a genial sense of humor. Far from being presented as the unscrupulous trafficker, Sholem Aleichem's hero comes across as a wolf dressed as a lamb—a cynical *caftan* that successfully deals in "furs", while keeping the attributes of a "gentleman."

The poor *shtetl* Jew who returns to his village as a rich merchant, but who boasts he can control the authorities, naturally provokes the suspicion of his interlocutor. Only when Mottke is about to get off the

train, his puzzled listener bursts out with the question he had been
meaning to ask since the beginning:

> "What, in short, is your business? What do you deal in?"
> "What do I deal in?" (He bursts out laughing.) "Not in prayer
> books, my friend, not in prayer books . . . "(140).

Sholem Aleichem's short story succeeds in suggesting rather than
revealing or offering a direct response. The elusive nature of the white
slave trafficker is glamourized and his real racket tempered through the
device of the self-portrait.

Leib Malach: (1894 - 1935)

The first time in Latin American history that such a critical and painful
issue as the white slave trade was written about in novels, or taken to
the stage, was with the work of Leib Malach (a pseudonym for Leib
Saltzman). Malach was a talented writer whose incendiary pages stirred
up the Jewish communities of Argentina and Brazil.[3] His career as a
journalist and dramatist started in Warsaw, where he contributed to an
important newspaper, *Der Varshever Togblat*. In 1919 Malach wrote
his first play, *Di Shvue* (The Oath) for the Jewish Workers' movement.
After his arrival in Argentina in 1922 he wrote for two Yiddish
newspapers, *Di Presse* and *Far Grois un Kleyn*, and in 1926 he became
a spokesman for the aggrieved immigrants of the Jewish agricultural
colonies of Brazil and Argentina—their *malach*, or angel. His exposé of
society's injustices extended into his fiction, which he used as a combat
arena to reform society.

Malach focused on the sordid sub-world of the Polish immigrant in
Brazil, a country that was of particular fascination for him. His Yiddish
naturalistic dramas *Opfal* and *Ibergus* (1926), just like his novel *Don
Domingo's Kraitzveg* (Don Domingo's Crossroads; 1930), deal with
the subject of the white slave trade.[4]

Ibergus, originally entitled "Gassn Freuen" (Women of the Street),
was translated from Yiddish into Spanish by Rosalía Rosembuj and
Nora Glickman under the title *Regeneración*. It premiered in 1926 at
the Politeama theater of Buenos Aires before a public of over two
thousand spectators.[5] When Doctor Mokdony reviewed the play in New
York on December 7, 1927, he wrote:

It is a play that describes a certain part of the Brazilian Jewish community. It is so faithfully naturalistic, and has such delicate and tender scenes that it keeps the public enchanted. When the curtain falls, after each act, one can hear tempestuous applause, not just of clapping hands but also of clapping hearts, and the feelings that this exciting play awakens.

The originality of *Ibergus* does not reside so much in its literary accomplishments, as in the controversy it provokes; it depicts a fight between the two components of the Jewish community. The success of the play is determined by its impact on the public, precisely because it deals with a subject that a large part of the Jewish community was trying hard to silence.[6]

The ideological furor *Ibergus* provoked among the Jews was stronger in Buenos Aires than in Poland. A month after it opened, on April 26, 1926, the play was rejected by the manager of a Yiddish theater in Buenos Aires who alleged that his public—consisting mostly of Jewish immigrants—would feel directly implicated in that affair. In fact, although Malach transferred the setting of his play to Rio de Janeiro, his condemnation of the prejudices and the hypocrisy of Jewish Argentine society was evident.

In the midst of this battle, Malach sent a compelling statement to *The Journal,* a newspaper published in New York. In his open letter he alerted the Jewish community of the impending dangers that threatened them, and informed them of the measures to avert those dangers. Yaacov Botoshansky remarks that "decent" Jews were separated from "indecent" Jews everywhere, except in the Jewish theater.[7] There, he stated, corrupt Jews made deals with some of the artists, who allowed them to have a direct influence on theater activities. With sharp objectivity Malach exposed some of their mistakes and judged his contemporaries for what they were: "a small, weak and defenseless bunch of Jews." Botoshansky further remarked that, although it was atypical of Malach to express himself in an alarmed fashion, he could not help commenting on the occasion of the premiere of his play: "if they are so afraid of *Ibergus,* it isn't enough to judge the play objectively. One should shout *guevald!* (Help!)."[8]

There soon began an open battle. Blood ran through the streets. The Jewish workers armed themselves with sticks and invaded the Jewish quarter determined to punish their vilified brothers, and expel them, if not from the city, at least from the Jewish Community. The war was fought in the streets, in the cafés, in the theaters, until finally the Jewish barrio became clean, worthy of those people who had come to build and to live an honest life (414).

In spite of the apparent victory of the traffickers who sponsored a great number of Jewish merchants in the capital, the fact is that they were never accepted within their community and that, to the end, they remained banned from all Jewish institutions. *Ibergus* combines an idyllic vision with harsh realism: Malach defines the two social worlds as the *Blate* (Yiddish for "impure": the prostitutes, the proprietors of the brothels, and an ex-trafficker who poses as a rabbi), and the *Vitishe*, which constitute the decent group of the population.

Malach situates *Ibergus* in Rio de Janeiro, a city where the white slave trade operated on a smaller scale than in Buenos Aires: Those *polacas* who had been directed to the port of Buenos Aires, but were considered of "lesser" value than others, were transported to Brazil. Also pimps and exploiters in trouble with the police used Rio de Janeiro as a "vacation center".

Reizl, the *polaca* heroine of *Ibergus* is portrayed as a victim of society who is destined to failure. Her rehabilitation as an honest woman is sought after by Rubio—a childhood friend—and by doctor Silva—a prominent Gentile lawyer who offers to marry her. Although Reizl is both frivolous and vain, she is also aware of the transitory nature of her beauty, and anguished about the consequences of her actions.

Significantly, Malach accentuates the differences between secular and religious Jews by opening his play on the eve of *Yom Kippur*. Reizl prefers to be labeled a "renegade" by the rest of the *polacas,* who insist on the importance of showing up early in the synagogue on the day of Atonement. She also refuses to pay the pimps the extortionist "contributions" they demand for building their own cemetery. She feels she has already given enough to her "brothers":

> Long years of sinking in my own pain. And they only came to collect the earnings. They've sucked my blood like vampires . . . (24).

What Reizl finds most abominable is that the *polacas* are not even buried in that cemetery: "Their flesh and their entrails rot, thrown away in the trash. What sister was buried as a human being?" (24) In her desire to obtain wealth and high social status, Reizl attempts to buy the respect of the Jewish community by refusing the sincere love of a poor immigrant actor, and by accepting instead the marriage proposal of Doctor Silva—an honorable Argentine politician. When Reizl is singled out at the theatre as an "undesirable" person, she is quick to take the blame:

> It was I, undoubtedly, who disturbed the peace of the ladies and
> gentlemen . . . I am a . . . here; take this. Look at my passbook. I am
> here illegally. Arrest, me, officer (33).

Expelled from the very same Jewish institutions that had accepted her, she adopts a melodramatic tone that characterizes Malach's entire play: "Do you see these ashes?", she asks, "They are my burnt dreams, the shambles of my hopes . . . " (40).

Reizl's last hope for salvation is placed on giving birth to a son, by Silva. Her disturbed condition makes her associate the horror at the murder of another prostitute with her own obsessive fears about terminating her pregnancy with an abortion:

> So many gold fingers! . . . So sharp . . . so pointed . . . they . . . they
> pluck out chunks under the skin . . . all eager to tear away . . . to
> rend . . . they are calling me from somewhere . . . they dig into my
> entrails (45).

As Reizl becomes a social outcast, she goes back to the brothel and, once again, turns into "everybody's woman". She succumbs without having been rehabilitated.

The dramatist's voice is heard through the words of El Rubio, Reizl's platonic lover, in charge of writing the Yiddish letters she sends to her family in Poland. Through Rubio, Malach also speaks for those well-meaning immigrants who struck root in America. That is why he passionately resents those Jews who bring shame to their community. Yet Rubio also expresses a larger fear that drives Jews to stick together: "We have to take care of ourselves, because there is always a threat from within and from without" (15). Fearing a break of Jewish paranoia, Rubio encourages his fellow Jews to fight against those

> henchmen who steal the innocent souls of their daughters and drive them to perdition . . . They are like a plague that covers us in this young, sun-lit country . . . This plague that sticks to our skins has become our burden . . . our cross" (32).

Doctor Silva, the National Deputy, is Malach's second *alter ego*. A fatherly, protective figure, he offers Reizl all he has. He even brings her family from Poland and learns some Yiddish words for their benefit. A devout Christian, Silva is witness to the spiritual change that takes place in Reizl, and goes so far as to identify her with the "sinner saint", the Virgin Mary. As a lawyer, Silva is a noble Creole who speaks up for the decent Jewish population. He tries to persuade the Argentine government, to expel the pimps, and enforce equality among all immigrants:

> The local population here is as multicolor as the sky over the mountains of Santa Teresa at sunset. And if there is even one man with a single stain in that racial melting pot, he will darken our horizon. Then he will be punished to the full extent of the law (14).

Malach was criticized because he did not silence Jewish prejudice in his writings. Through the character of Reizl's mother, Peseleh, Malach manifests the worst racial biases among Jews. Although she is led to believe Doctor Silva is Jewish, Pesele suspects he is not. Coming from Poland, a country that discriminates against gypsies, she insists that Doctor Silva's dark skin makes him "worse than a gypsy" (22), and never considers that, thanks to Silva, her daughter has a chance to be saved from prostitution.

Malach also condemns the intransigence of Jewish leaders in Buenos Aires, and their inability to extirpate the "impure" element from their midst. The contrast between the "decent" group and the pimps represented by Kvoke, their president, increases when they meet face to face. Malach presents Kvoke as a religious fanatic, a morally and physically decrepit sorceress who uses her intelligence for advancement in the brothel. On the one hand Kvoke pushes Reizl to use her influence in favor of her girls, so that Dr. Silva will help them; on the other hand she presses Reizl to abort Silva's son, a "black bastard".

Jalaf, a reformed ex-trafficker, also scorns those who alienate him. Having become an "honest" businessman, he demands respectability for his entire family. When he is denied entrance to the Yiddish theatre, he takes his revenge by accusing everybody of being anarchist. With such a denunciation the immigrants run the risk of being deported and denaturalized, as many foreigners were.

The tensions between the *Vitishe* and the *Blate*, the two social rivals, are best seen when the spectators are present at a Yiddish play entitled: "A real man". Stare, who plays the leading role in the play is at the last moment replaced by an amateur actor.[9] In his speech Stare argues that an actor is supposed to "sell his art to whoever wishes to buy it," just like a salesman sells his merchandise. But he clashes against the intolerance of the public that does not admit any reconciliation.

The previous attempts to close the doors of the theaters to the undesirables had been resisted by their owners, who could profit from the attendance of the pimps, and specially from the exploited women, for whom the Yiddish theater was a favorite pastime.

In his novel *Don Domingo's Crossroads*, situated in Rio de Janeiro, Malach again exposes the two warring factions: the "pure", and the "impure". Each of the six-parts of the novel—"Wild Grass"; "The Kaufmans", "Palm Trees"; "The Yellow Shadow"; "The Host in Town"; "The Crossroad"—can be read independently of the others. The section entitled "The Yellow Shadow" depicts in great detail the life of Jews connected with the prostitution ring: it follows their intrigues, betrayals, and struggles against the respectable elements of the Jewish community. *Don Domingo's Crossroads* describes the adventures of Lobus Donie, a Polish youth who comes to Rio de Janeiro, falls into the hands of the "indecent" element, and becomes an exploiter of women. And still, Domingo retains some conventional ethical values. As Lobus Donie he finally becomes a revolutionary, participates in the Brazilian civil war, and dies in the struggle.

The novel excels in its detailed description of Jewish types: believers and atheists, pimps, madams, and innocent victims, moving between the Old World and Latin America. The Yiddish theater—with its idiosyncratic artists and its demanding spectators—comes to life in these pages. Malach's descriptions have been justifiably compared with

Sholem Asch. Some passages are lyrical, like the one of the love between Juana, the Christian-mulatto prostitute, and Don Domingo.

Melech Ravich, a contemporary critic, held the opinion that some lines of Malach's novels "are among the best in Yiddish literature," particularly because of his insights into Jewish immigration in a far away land."[10]

> Jewish immigrants can be found at every corner of the world. They get rich, they get poor. But their presence is not recorded in Jewish literature. Nothing is known, in particular, about the Jewish community of Brazil. With Malach's touch, the novel becomes still more valuable. One often hears of the "universal dimension" of Yiddish literature. Malach's novel undoubtedly is largely responsible for that universal dimension . . . While there are many narrators in world literature, there are very few in Yiddish literature. Malach is one of them. I am not exaggerating when I state that the translation of Malach's work would bring much honor to Yiddish literature. An entire gallery of types parades in front of the astonished reader. Malach is capable of mustering a profound knowledge of the shame that humanity stores, and in particular, of the underworld of Jewish traffickers. In a brutal, naked style he describes their viciousness, their immorality (315-316).

Malach's description of the orgy on Yom Kippur Eve at the cemetery of the *t'meyim* is so colorful and eloquent, that it can be compared to the best writings of Scholem Asch. In the scene in which Don Domingo takes Juana back to his little East European village, Juana is portrayed more like a saint than a prostitute. Her love for Don Domingo is one of the most moving passages in Yiddish literature.

Isaac Bashevis Singer: (1904-1992)

Isaac Bashevis Singer was fascinated with the clandestine aspect of the *polacas*. Since his work follows that of his predecessors Sholem Aleichem and Sholem Asch, Singer's writings convey an atmosphere of irreality along with a search for faithfulness and truth in the troubled condition of his characters. In two of his stories, the protagonist, a Jewish American writer on tour through South America, lectures in Yiddish to his Polish compatriots. In *The Colony* the narrator is led on a tour of Buenos Aires by Sonia, a Polish immigrant residing there.[11] Through her he finds out about the battles that took place between the traffickers and the leaders of Argentine Jewry, as well as of the efforts of the latter to rid themselves of the criminal elements by denying them access to their institutions. The girl recalls the early days when the traffickers, the "impure", played a central role in the Jewish community, excercizing their power by controling the Yiddish theater and by forcing young Jewish women into prostitution:

> They owned the Yiddish theater. When they didn't like a play, they took it out of circulation. But the rest of the community kept away from them . . . Many of the old men had once been pimps, and their wives prostitutes. In those days, when the traffickers were in power, they tried to take advantage of any woman who was alone: They had specially assigned men to seduce them" (209-210).

In spite of having spent many years in Argentina and of having familiarized herself with the details of Jewish life there, Sonia is not acquainted with the customs of the Christian majority. This reflects, perhaps, Singer's own ignorance of Argentine customs and people. Sonia affirms, for example, that "all Argentines are Spaniards" (almost two centuries after Argentina gained independence from Spain) and she makes generalizations about the machista influence which the Argentinians exert over their milieu: "They have many churches where only their women go in to pray. Every Spaniard has a wife and a lover" (210).

In *Hanka*, I.B. Singer's second story on the subject of the *polacas*, like in *The Colony*, the mood fluctuates between dream and reality.[12] The narrator, established in America, recounts the experiences of his tour to Argentina with the purpose of lecturing in Yiddish, as that is the language he has in common with his Eastern European correligionists. Several strange events take place from the beginning of his trip. The narrator is obsessed with memories from Poland and with fantasies he had hidden away. Hanka, his Argentine guide, is one of the ghosts of his past that comes back to frighten him: a specter of the Holocaust. During a visit to the Jewish cemetery assigned to Jewish pimps and prostitutes, the narrator recalls that when he was a child, he had heard horrid stories about those poor women who were deceived with false promises of marriage; then put in chains, and sold in an auction as soon as they reached the port of Buenos Aires. If a girl resisted, she was beat down by her seducer, who tore up her hair and stuck pins under her fingernails. What else was the poor thing to do? She was sold to a brothel and had to do whatever the client wanted. Sooner or later, a tiny worm entered her blood, and she could not live much longer. After seven years her hair and teeth fell out. Her nose rotted away and that was the end of the drama. Since she was corrupt, she was buried behind the fence.—Alive?! (14).

The narrator recalls that the last interjection requesting clarification of the "alive?", was asked by an awe-stricken child, like the one he was when he first heard of this traffick. Yet many years later, as he stands in front of the tombs of the "fallen" women, the same sensation of horror overpowers him. Singer's stories illustrate the superstitious beliefs, coupled with the lack of news that fed the imagination about the nature of prostitution in Argentina.

In his novel *Scum* (1991) Singer despicts a the life of Max, a character who after forty seven years in Poland decides to emigrate to Argentina, where he conducts sinister operations. The unexpected death of his son, followed by his wife's madness, prompts him to return to Warsaw. There he intends to recapture a decent existence that had been slipping through his fingers. But the year was 1906, and Poland was a nest of poverty and corruption. In *Scum* I.B. Singer details the subworld of the white slave traffick, of falsification of documents, and of illegal brewing of alcohol, in other words, of absolute immorality.

II. THE WHITE SLAVE TRADE IN LATIN AMERICAN FICTION:[15]

At the same time as Yiddish theater flourishes in Argentina, the dramatic genre that best reflects the immigrant's trauma is the *sainete*, a one-act comic sketch. By the 1920s, the number of short farces that deal with the immigrant's conflict in confrontation with the creole in a vast and hostile metropolis, reaches the thousands. One of the sainetes of Alberto Novión deals with the white slave trade. Many of the sainetes were used to introduce a rich variety of songs, of tangos in particular. Tango practices, in fact, originated in the brothels, the site of an extensive repertoire of tango lyrics. The *Zwi Migdal* organization grew mostly during the years when the tango flourished. The titles of the tangos of those years serve to illustrate the musical correspondences with the demimonde: *El Cafishio* (The Pimp) by Iriarte Cavanesi, 1918); *Carne de cabaret* (Flesh of the Cabaret) by Roldán-Lambertucci, 1920); *Garabita*, by Contursi-Terés, 1926); *Mano cruel* (Cruel hand) by Tagini-Mutarelli, 1928; *Muñeca brava* (Wild doll) by Cadícamo Visca; 1928); *Acquaforte* by Marambio Catán-Petorossi, 1891). The tango was witness on its path of crime, when innocent women were sold in auctions to the highest bidder. When the white slave expanded through the interior of the country, the *canfinfleros* (pimps) had become professional traffickers who were protected by a powerful organization. The Buenos Aires *Cafiolo* (another slang term for pimp) worked independently and meant to spend his earnings in his favorite passtimes: gambling, fancy dressing, barber-shops, cafés and horse-racing. An excerpt from a poem by Enrique Cadícamo illustrates how the tango reflected the mood in the bordello: "The pianola pierced through the tango rolls. Picaresque movies heated up the atmosphere. And from the patio, the voice of a pimp reciting a vulgar song was heard. When from some room you could hear the madam yelling in Polish. It sounded like a slap on the behind of the girl who happened to be idle." (*Viento que lleva y trae*).[14]

Alberto Novión:

El cambalache de Petroff ("Petroff's Junkshop"; 1937) a comic play by Alberto Novión that premiered in 1920, traces the profile of the Russian immigrant—a ruinous, despicable stereotype—who is prepared to sell his own daughter to a so called *caftan*, (a long black robe worn by Jews from Eastern Europe), in exchange for personal gain.[15] But the young woman, already a Creole, refuses to become "a merchandise of a pawnshop" and falls in love with a gentile Argentinian who saves her from her father. The outcome is a happy one, and the young couple triumphs.

Julián Martel: (1967-1896)

La bolsa (The Stock Exchange; 1891), a novel by Juan María Miró, better known by his pseudonym of Julián Martel, has now become a classic of Argentine literature. Published in the conservative newspaper

La Nación, Martel labeled this fictional account "a social study"; it introduced an antisemitic theme that has influenced nationalistic authors up to the present day. In Martel's view the Jews embodied the faults and vices of all foreigners. They controlled the world of financial speculations; they were the "extortionists," the "vampires of modern society" who struck easy deals and reaped exorbitant profits, and promoted corruption among "naive public officials." The "diabolical" characters were, consequently, also responsible for the slave trade. Martel's Jewish figure, Filiberto Mackser, is an odious stereotype, both in his repulsive appearance and in his sinister character. Posing as jewelry dealer, Mackser manages "to cover up his infamous traffic and to give an appearance of respectability to his continuous trips abroad" (53). The real purpose of his trips, however, is to procure prostitutes. Martel makes indirect reference to the *Zwi Migdal*, presided over by Mackser, as a "club of human flesh traffickers, located next to the police station, which the police had never dared disturb" (53).[16] Through Mackser, Martel puts in evidence the open complicity that existed between traffickers and the people who held official posts, carrying out illicit transactions in all the governmental echelons.

Manuel Gálvez: (1882-1962)

While Martel's antisemitism, uninfluenced by contact with flesh-and-blood Jews, deliberately ignored the campaign launched by the Jewish community in Buenos Aires to wipe out the *Zwi Migdal*, Manuel Gálvez did praise Jewish efforts to eradicate the bad elements from their midst by denying them entry into their synagogues and burial in their cemeteries. Gálvez, a conservative Catholic novelist was the author of thirty novels— two of them about prostitution: *Nacha Regules* (1919) and *Historia de arrabal* (The Story of a Slum, 1923). Gálvez had become an expert on the subject of prostitution after having written a play as a young student, *La hija de Atenor* (Atenor's Daughter, 1903), which became the basis for *Historia de arrabal*, and a law thesis entitled "The White Slave Trade" (1905). Donna Guy observes that although his research documents the existence of foreign traffickers who bribe local authorities in their corrupted activities, and although he recounts tragic stories of deception and cruelty toward foreign women forced to engage in prostitution in Argentina, the prostitutes and the pimps portrayed in his fiction are principally native-

born Argentines.[17] His novel *Nacha Regules* depicts the miserable state
of prostitutes in Buenos Aires.[18] Gálvez' sympathies are obviously with
the "muchachas de la vida" (fast women). He commiserates with the
polacas "who were sold in public auctions, who were brutalized and
deeply hurt" (28), and describes in detail the activities of a clandestine
net in Buenos Aires, while observing how "the traffickers used to
deceive the girls in Austria and in Russia", and how Buenos Aires had
become "a human flesh market." (28) The novel conveys a clear moral
message: Nacha (Ignacia) Regules is not a victim of white slavery, but
of a love affair with a Creole who loses his money and his health when
his aspirations of reforming society fail him. When Nacha repents of
her sins she is saved.

Gálvez was a political skeptic who doubted the effectiveness of
revolution and even of social reform. He regarded himself as a true
Catholic and was surprised at the harsh criticism directed at his writings
by other Catholic intellectuals who did not percieve that *Nacha Regules*
was a deeply Catholic novel, and that it stood as a statement of personal
spiritual salvation.

Moral salvation and religion are central to Gálvez' second realist
novel, *Historia de arrabal.* His lack of hope in the effectiveness of a
social revolution is reflected in the tragic outcome of the action. By the
early 1920's Gálvez was not yet prepared to device a harmonious
relationship between Linda Corrales, a victim of rape and forced
prostitution, and Daniel Forti, an anarchist. The path of the lovers is
strewn with obstacles throughout the novel and the relationship ends in
disaster. The heroine murders her lover and patron, the only man who
could have pulled her out of her predicament.

A more romantic view of the *polaca* emerged in the writings of
liberal, socially conscious authors who showed the prostitute as a
victim. These include Samuel Eichelbaum and David Viñas, whose
sympathy for the *polacas* and whose sensitivity to anti-Semitism may
have been related to their own Jewish origins.

Samuel Eichelbaum: (1894–1967)

In all his dramas Samuel Eichelbaum is concerned about the destiny of
victims who suffer grave deceptions in life; in *Nadie la conoció nunca*
(No one ever knew her; 1945) he criticizes the cultural attitudes of the
privileged class.[19] Here Eichelbaum observes the anguished life of

Ivonne, a *polaca* crushed by society and dragged into the "easy" life, is a true victim of social circumstance and an outcast. Ivonne hides her real identity behind a French name, which is better appreciated by the Creoles than other foreign names. Such a name also serves to improve Ivonne's professional status as a prostitute, and to protect her from persecution as a Jew. In this play Eichelbaum alludes to the incidents of the Tragic Week of 1919, when Jews were used as scapegoats during a conflict between the workers and the police. He connects these incidents with the pogroms that provoked the flight of thousands of Jews from Russia. The state of unrest in which Ivonne is depicted to be living in Buenos Aires is, in Tiempo's view, that of all prostitute women, and it is also that of all humiliated men, who suffer from the hostility of the native Argentinians on account of their Jewish religion.

The joviality of the first act of the play turns serious when Ivonne hears a group of young Argentinian aristocrats—her clients and her lover, Ricardito—boast of having shaved off the beard of a Jewish immigrant, publicly degrading him. In her own living room Ivonne witnesses a playful reenactment of the shaving, performed by the perpetrators. Responding to his racial insult, she strikes one of the offenders, thus demonstrating that she still retains some feeling for her origins. The realization that they had done this for amusement shocks Ivonne into recovering her Jewish identity. It also brings back memories of her father, murdered during the Tragic Week of 1919, when a pogrom broke out in the streets of Buenos Aires. Recalling similar pogroms in Russia, which had caused her to emigrate to Argentina, Ivonne expresses her remorse in a confession of her error:

> I am glad . . . that my father did not live to see me leading this life of
> debauchery. I thank my stars that I never had to face him looking like
> this. Even worse, today I feel the emptiness of my whole life, like a
> terrible revelation (56).

As a redeemed heroine, Ivonne sees herself as a representative of all Jewish women. She feels compelled to behave with dignity "Because now, in each of us, in our words and our deeds, the [Jewish] race prevails"(56). Her curse is that despite her understanding, she is too weak to change and will remain a prostitute.

David Viñas: (1929)

Like Eichelbaum, Viñas links violence with casual amusement. In his novel *En la semana trágica* (During the Tragic Week; 1974) he exposes the thoughtless brutality of the "guardias blancas" (white guards) who went on a rampage of murder and destruction against the Jewish community in 1919.[20] Violence that week was an entertainment for the well-to-do youth, who alternated between whoring with the *polacas* and the *francesas*, and beating up defenseless Jews. In a later novel, *Los dueños de la tierra* (The Owners of the Land; 1974),[21] Viñas's protagonist, Vicente, remembers that he and his fellow law students used to leave the courthouse and amuse themselves "with the *polacas* or with the Jewesses, who after all were the same thing" (69). When he compares the different sorts of women he has encountered, Vicente finally decides that , contrary to public opinion, "one Jewess is worth four Frenchwomen anytime"(69). Significantly, both Viñas and Eichelbaum create male protagonists who, despite their expressed hatred for Jews, eventually fall in love with, and marry Jewish women; yet this resolves none of their internal tensions.

Alicia Muñoz:

Similar events plagued the city of Rosario, until the annulment of the Social Profilaxis law in 1933.[22] In *Las crónicas de Pichincha* (The Pichincha Chronicles) Alicia Muñoz points out the feminine perspective through the dialogues between the prostitutes who carry out their duty in an independent fashion, and those who survive at the mercy of a trafficker. As an echo to the verses of Sor Juana Inés de la Cruz, who already in 1537 defied men by questioning who is more to blame, "la que peca por la paga o el que paga por pecar," (the one who sins for pay or the one who pays in order to sin), one of the characters of *Las crónicas de Pichincha* cries out against the hypocrisy of men and concludes bitterly:

> . . . if it not were for us, they would go like dogs on the streets raping old women and school girls . . . Hell, what a crummy race man is. They throw your head into the shit and afterwards they want to rehabilitate you (11).

César Tiempo: (1906-1980)

Perhaps the most humane outlook on this subject is that of *Versos de una* . . . (Verses of a . . .), by César Tiempo, whose pseudonym was Israel Zeitlin.[23] In recent years the poems began to be reevaluated for their social significance; but in 1926, when they were first published, Tiempo decided to play a practical joke on his fellow writers, and hid behind a third pseudonym—that of Clara Béter.[24] Appropriately, Tiempo quotes Jesus' words from the New Testament in the epigraph: "Aquel de vosotros que se halle exento de pecado que arroje la primera piedra" (May he who is free from guilt cast the first stone).

Although Tiempo is best known for his avant-garde poetry—most popular in Argentina during the 1920's and 30's—and for his socially committed literature, his *Verses of a* . . . was a successful hoax in which he convinced his public that he had a discovered the verses written by a Ukranian white-slave, Clara Béter, who was a consummate poet. Before it became known that the author of the collection was Tiempo himself, the *Verses of a* . . . had gone through five editions.

To increase the author's credibility, Tiempo dedicated the book to Tatiana Pavlova, an Italian-Russian actress who was enjoying a successful season in Buenos Aires. In "Patio de la infancia" (Childhood yard) Clara Béter evokes a faraway past in a Ukranian village where she and "Katiushka" were childhood friends, and she reflects on the outcome of that friendship:

Mas pasaron los años y nos llevó la vida/ por distintos senderos. /
Yo . . . soy una cualquiera.

(But the years passed and life carried us / along different paths. /
I . . . am a nobody.)

The poems show Clara Béter in all her contradictions. At times she is proud of her body and pleased of the attraction she evokes in men. At other times she feels repugnance for men who prey on her body, and is overwhelmed by hopelessness: In "Presentimiento" (Premonition) she asks herself: "¿Terminaré mi vida en un prostíbulo?" (Will my days end in a brothel?) and, again, in "Fatalidad" (Fate) she repeats the same question: "¿Tendré lugar, cariño, sosiego, algún día? / Y una voz recóndita responde: Jamás." (Will I have a place, love, peace some day? And a hidden voice responds: Never.) Accepting her fate, she becomes optimistic and wishes for a son:

> Si tuviera un hijo, cómo lo amaría! / Con su alba inocencia purificaría / mi carne de venta la dulce criatura . . .
>
> Yo le enseñaría que santa o ramera/ la que engendra un hijo / no es más que una mujer." ("Mancer")

> (If I had a son, how much I would love him! / With his white innocence that sweet creature I would purify /my flesh that is for sale . . . / I would teach him that saint or whore / she who conceives a son / is merely woman.)

In tracing the steps towards the creation of a myth around Clara Béter (beter for bitter), Esther Irizarry recounts that at the time Tiempo was only 17 years old, and that the 100,000 copies sold proved its enormous success. For the author's contemporaries, the work had biographical value: today's readers can appreciate the confessions of an artistically gifted prostitute objectively, as a sincere and convincing creation.

Fifty years after its publication, the *Versos de una . . .* had fallen into oblivion. Irizarry reflects that the apparent sincerity that initially seduced so many readers, turned to disillusion when they realized that this was an impostor's creation from an otherwise respectable writer.

Tiempo deliberately employs the name of a female author with the intention of exposing the feelings of the brothels' victims suffering from the injustices of society, but forgotten in anonymity. The heroine never lacks opportunities to remember her past in Europe with nostalgia. Through the poetry, the protagonist finds liberation from her tormented reality, and laments having lost the chance of becoming one day, a mother and wife worthy of respect.

In spite of the positive metaphors of bread, sun, and water, the recurrent leitmotif of this collection is that of deceit. Clara is torn between the contrast of what she is—a sensitive poet—and what she does for a living. Both "Vida" (Life), and "Amorío ciudadano" (Urban love) deal with mutual deceit. A man treats her like an innocent bride while she pours out words of love in return: "Mutuamente nos hemos engañado." Deeply moved by the qualities of sincerity, piety and humility that characterize Clara Béter's verses, Elías Castelnuovo wrote in the introduction to "her" work:

> Clara Béter is the voice of anguish that comes from the brothel. Her verses vindicate all infamous women. . .[they] bring a new element to our literature: piety. . .Clara Béter. . .does not protest: The people who look at her protest. . . This woman distinguishes herself completely from other women who write because she is incredibly sincere.[25]

In spite of his illusionist rhetoric, César Tiempo is not a romantic author. He aspires to transform society with his protest: the narrator, as a prostitute, identifies with the miserable fate of the unknown worker; piously, she comforts him: "You who suffer so, deserve the ephemeral feast that my body is willing to offer you" (p 29).

Los versos de una . . . echoes the voices of those fallen women who feel repugnance towards a world that is indifferent to their pain: "How you disgust me, you vulture-claws! . . . and still, one is expected to smile . . . " (38). The protagonist is particularly violent when she expresses the thirst for vengeance that women feel towards those who exploit them: "I'd give anything to drown them all in one vomit!" (42). But her rage is only verbal. She remains basically passive, suffers without rebelling, and does not seek revenge in the face of degradation.

Leonardo Senkman in *La identidad judía en la literatura argentina* observes that Clara Béter's account of her life as a Jewish prostitute in Buenos Aires provides an accurate composite of social realities during Tiempo's times.[26]

Eager to encourage fan mail from admirers of his ideal woman, Tiempo went as far as to give Clara Béter an address in Rosario, Santa Fé. Years later, however, Tiempo was finally forced to admit that he instigated the Clara Béter deception: "That prostitute created a male prostitute. I was that male prostitute".[27]

In 1985 the novelist and critic David Viñas raised fresh controversies over *Versos* by speaking of Tiempo's collection as equal in significance to Ricardo Guiraldes' novel *Don Segundo Sombra* (1926)—long considered a masterpiece of Argentine literature.[28]

Some fifty years later Tiempo evoked his literary farce in *Clara Béter y otras fatamorganas,* for which he invented a daughter to Clara Béter that would justify and vindicate her mother's name. Estelle Irizarry observes that the new character's tone is cynical and devoid of sensitivity. Yet, in it, the daughter defends the dignity of the profession of the prostitute: "Everyone charges for their work in this consuming society. Most other women make a smaller sacrifice and they get paid better." In a joking manner, the daughter predicts that Clara Béter will speak up one day, and that César Tiempo would be remembered as "un poeta de la gran puta"—a pun for "a hell of a poet" as well as for "a poet of the great whore".

As in *Sabatión argentino* and in other poetic works, César Tiempo attributes to Clara Béter some characteristics of the Jewish race, such as her frugal nature that provides for her little sister, back in the *shtetl,* "con estas manos que recogen dinero del barro" (with these hands that pick up money from the mud). He also attributes Clara's longings for sisterhood and brotherhood—"hermana-hermano"—to her feelings of compassion, pain, and hope for humanity. In "Atavismos" she proposes

> . . . dar las gracias a mi raza judía / que me ha hecho ahorrativa . . .
> Hoy debemos sufrir . . . para nosotras / esa es la ley suprema de la
> vida . . . pero el futuro puede ser en nuestras manos dócil arcilla.
> /Modelemos entonces las estatuas de nuestro porvenir, hermanas
> mías.

> (. . . to give thanks to my Jewish race / that has made me thrifty . . .
> Today we must suffer . . . for us / that is the supreme law of life . . .
> but the future can become docile clay in our hands. Let us then, my
> sisters, model the statues of our future).

If Clara Béter is a wandering Jewess, like the wandering Jew of "Itinerario", she drags the itinerant heart of her life as an errant daughter of the Diaspora, who suffers with bitterness the expulsion from Paradise. Clara Béter is orphan of parents and orphan of the Sabbath, which for Tiempo is the essence of the Nation. Clara Béter's trauma is that of immigration and of poverty—an outcast deprived of respect and compassion, alienated from her native town and from her Argentine village.

Mario Szichman: (1945)

During the 1970's literary accounts of Jewish prostitution became more realistic, their scope more ambitious, and their characters more three-

dimensional. Cases in point are the Argentinian novelist Mario
Szichman and the Brazilian Moacyr Scliar. Both trace a composite
picture of the Jewish prostitute, whose career turns her from a naive
immigrant into an experienced madam of a brothel. Szichman writes in
a bitter, sarcastic vein. His autobiographical novels, linked to his
Jewish heritage are cynical, less conciliatory than those of earlier
authors. In his novel *A las 20:25 la señora entró en la inmortalidad*
("At 20:25 The Lady Entered Immortality") (1981), Dora, the madam of
a brothel raises questions about the real motivation of women who end
up in her profession, and about the extent to which they are victimized
by men.[29] A continuing character in several of Szichman's novels, Dora
is a hardened, resourceful, unscrupulous woman who becomes a
prostitute in Buenos Aires to save herself from starvation: "I discovered
that the world belonged to men, and since I could not conquer it with
my head, I used my *tooches* (backside)."

In her Yiddishized Spanish, Dora does not make any distinction
between obscenity and refinement, as long as she gets what she wants.
She has no qualms about openly acknowledging the link between crime
and prostitution: "There was a certain *polaca* who whistled at the client,
and lured him into the passage . . . there they would take away his ring,
his watch, his wallet." Dora cynically models herself on the
melodramatic heroines of tangos and milongas, as she retells the story
of her life:

> I don't go rolling around from here to there as I used to. There is
> luxury in my room. I spend as much as I wish. And no one reminds
> me that, once upon a time, I was the mud of the delta, the easy ride
> who was mocked on nights of carousing and champagne.

Dora is presented as a cynical and vulgar woman who becomes a
prostitute, motivated by ambition and poverty. The only chance she
finds to attain social status is by becoming a procuress. Dora's drive to
succeed as a madam is based on her conclusion that prostitutes who are
uncooperative and unenthusiastic about their work can never get ahead.
In her estimation, "I knew what was in store for me . . . and wasn't
going to let myself fall just like that . . . to be a *curveh* (prostitute) was
just a step in the business, to become what I am today." Since she must
be a prostitute, Dora is determined to be a good one. Her cynicism
dominates her conversations with her clients. At the same time as she is

performing her job, she portrays herself as a victim of corrupt social institutions and claims that prostitution "is a monstrous slavery, tolerated by society, regulated by the state and protected by the police." Her cynicism is best illustrated in a conversation she holds with one of her clients who attempts to give her a word of warning:

> They will infect you with horrible illnesses, you will fall even lower . . . that is what awaits you if you don't change your life-style.

> Sí, sí . . . I want to be different. And you will help me; you who are so good. How do you prefer, up or down?

Dora fully agrees with Elma, a friend and model of a madam, that "we Yidn are not like the *goyim*; there is always the *moral issue*." The "moral issue" is not so much moral as it is a desire to maintain ethnicity—to maintain Jewishness in a Catholic world.

Paradoxically, although Dora exploits the *polacas* and debases them to a condition of "merchandise", she still keeps her contact with them through their religion, arguing that morality is always a vital issue with them (136). In order to survive as a Jew in a foreign culture, Dora herself abides by ethical and moral rules, and she also takes advantage of them. But as a madam, Dora does not pretend to be naive or even cynical any longer. She judges harshly the institutions that publicly absolve from responsibility those girls who consider themselves victims of society.

> "They always talk of the losers," Dora thought, "but they forget the others. Just because we are just a few, maybe? But can all be generals in a battle? I'd wish just one of them [women] would come to me and tell me she was forced to do it. Just one. They beg us to give them work. Sometimes they have to be kicked out. And what's worse, they always come back. They are all stupid and greedy. And they wear everything they own. They don't even have five *tzent*. One has to teach them how to walk, how to behave. How many come out of it married: liars, selfish, unkempt. One has to watch them with everything. Or they get fat, or ill, or careless. "

Although Dora pretends to be indifferent to the rejection of the *polacas* in the Yiddish theater and to their segregation in the Jewish cemetery, she takes comfort in the fact that they are still part of the Jewish community.

Israel Chas de Cruz:

Szichman is not alone among the writers who depict how the prostitutes were not the victims but the victimizers. One of the stories of *Picaresca criolla* by Chas de Cruz (1966), entitled "Enigmatic Adventure," portrays a credulous client who is hopelessly deceived by the prostitutes who lure him to their establishment.[30]

Moacyr Scliar: (1937–)

Like the rest of the literature reviewed here, Moacyr Scliar in *O ciclo das águas* (*The Cycle of Waters*, 1978) makes use of historical, documented material on the subject of prostitution in Argentina and Brazil as a "point of departure." Scliar sets his novel in Porto Alegre, one of the cities in Brazil to where the white slave trade moved after being driven out of Buenos Aires. *O ciclo das águas* presents nostalgic reminiscences of the *shtetl* existence: the dire poverty of Polish families, and the naivete of parents who entrusted daughters to unscrupulous men, believing the claims of pious orthodoxy and the false promises of marriage made by the *caftans* and their agents. Scliar states that Esther Markowitz, the protagonist, is based on a real person who was born and raised in Poland.[31] In the novel, after Esther's arranged marriage to a Jew who turns out to be a pimp, she is introduced to the brothel life in Paris. Here all her contacts—and clients—speak to her in Yiddish as well as French and Polish. Esther is first humiliated and then seduced by the wealth and the easy life that surrounds her. Scliar seems to follow Albert Londres' course in the unfolding of events, turning his euphemistic terminology into dramatic action: "A *husband* dies, his *widow* is doing well, he assigns her to one of his trusted lieutenants." In this novel, when Esther's husband Mendele dies, his "widow" is assigned to Luis el malo," or Leiser, the Latin American chief of the *Zwi Migdal* organization.

The title of the novel, which translates as "The Cycle of Waters," symbolizes the rebirth of Esther in her illegitimate son, Marcos. This parallel between the chemical composition of the waters and the human reproductive cycle runs through the novel, for it is through Marcos that Esther regains her respectability. She sends her son away from her "house" in order to have him brought up as a proper Jewish boy, has him circumcised, and sees that he attains Bar Mitzvah. It is through Marcos that Esther expiates her guilt for having been a prostitute and for having failed her father, a *mohel* (ritual circumciser) in Poland. Throughout her life, Esther learns to cope with the unjust, painful realities of the world. Whether she is portrayed as the victimized woman struggling for independence and respectability, as the attractive "Queen Esther of America," or as the Frenchified Madame Mark (née Markowitz), Scliar's heroine never completely loses her dignity. She emerges from her painful trials as a proud, sensitive woman.

The fetid waters drunk by the children of Santa Lucía, a slum in Porto Alegre, become a revealing metaphor for Scliar. Despite the danger of contamination, despite the infected environment, the children of Santa Lucía grow up healthy. Marcos becomes a professor of biology. Studying in his laboratory, he views the polluted waters through a microscope, discovering each impurity and reporting it to his students. Marcos himself, born of a woman infected with syphilis, escapes unscathed and free of disease.

Esther's illegitimate son stands as a spokesman for middle-class values and human rights. He is deeply concerned about the corruption of Brazilian politicians who neglect the poor, about the stagnant university system which does not educate, and about land speculators who trample on the weak and disenfranchised. The social ills, in Marcos' opinion, are far worse than prostitution.

III. THE WHITE SLAVE TRADE IN CINEMA:

The four films discussed here—Asesinato *en el Senado (Assassination at the Senate), Camino del sur (Heading South), Last Embrace* and *Tango desnudo (Naked Tango)*—provide fictional depictions of the *polacas* and original perceptions of the White Slave Trade. Almost three generations removed from the actual events in the 1930s in Europe and in Argentina, the directors have established new perspectives on the political and social conditions that prevailed at the time, such as the corruption by the official authorities of governmental agencies, and the blatant exploitation of women immigrants who made their own way to Buenos Aires.

Although some of the characters can be easily recognized as stereotypes within the sub-world of white slavery, it is clear that present day observers tend to portray women in the prostitution business as victims at the mercy of ruthless pimps and procurers who took advantage of the lack of leadership in the country. At the turn of the century Argentina's immigrants were a majority of the population.

Asesinato en el senado (1984), directed by Juan Jusid takes place in Argentina of the 1930s. It centers around the corrupt political climate of the country that led to the murder attempt on Senator Lisandro de la Torre, one of the few enlightened senators who spoke in the name of democracy. The film emphasizes the contrast between the newly arrived under-age *polaquita*—milk white skin, blue eyes, submissive— and the rest of the prostitutes, who look older, professional, and well adjusted to their jobs. The madam in charge of the bordello is depicted as a sly businesswoman whose real loyalty is to a clientele that allows her to keep her establishment open in a residential area of Buenos Aires. Her concern for the welfare of her "girls" is only determined by the amount of profits she derives from them.

Asesinato en el Senado directs its condemnation towards the widespread corruption in some factions of the Argentine government and their manipulation of foreign affairs, specifically regarding the exportation of refrigerated meats. Great Britain's economic policy towards Argentina, and the generous profits it derived from its transactions, is presented as another form of economic exploitation, on a par with the political and social corruption in the country. Senator Lisandro de la Torre was the first to expose the complicity between the British and Argentine land-owning politicians through the falsified classification of meats. The Argentine farmers were cheated out of the profits made by exporting first quality meat as second grade. The difference was kept by the middle man and by the *hacendados*, who took advantage of their political connections and manipulated government regulations at the Senate.

In Jusid's film the "meat" sold to foreign markets stands as a metaphor for the women sold as "food" or as "merchandise" at the brothels. While most of the prostitutes portrayed in this film are adult women, the *polaca* is here a fifteen-year old girl who does not understand any Spanish and is forced to comply with the perverse whims of her customers. This *polaca* is brutalized by a hood. Jusid establishes a parallel between the prostitute who is brutalized by a corrupted individual, and Argentina—a country of immigrants—which is desecrated by local politicians.

On a par with the *polaca* is the left-oriented proletariat which opposes General Uriburu's presidency. When the workers complain of the corruption and the abuses and threaten to strike, they are savagely tortured by the thugs in the service of criminal politicians. In the 1930s, in fact, Argentina first started experimenting with the use of electric cattle prods on human beings. The film suggests that the cruelty against those who dared defy the authorities is as ruthless as that used against the *polacas* in the bordello.

The action of *Asesinato en el Senado* alludes to the new "morality campaign" that was launched in Argentina in 1934—without lasting success—after the long period of corruption under Uriburu's military dictatorship. During this time honest judges attempted to impose new morality laws by prohibiting prostitution and closing down many brothels. Senator De la Torre's suicide follows soon after the cold-blooded murder of his supporter, Dr. Enzo Bardevere, when he was trying to shield a bullet aimed the senator during a Senate session in Buenos Aires with his body. In spite of the high popularity De la Torre enjoyed among the masses, his suicide reflects the senator's desperate response to his inability to bring meaningful change to the Senate.

The second feature, *Camino del Sur*, directed by Juan Bautista Stagnaro follows the *polaca* from her native village in Poland to Argentina. Here the stereotypes move within a realistic framework. The brothel—located in La Boca, a poor district of Buenos Aires—is sometimes entirely flooded and the entire operation has to be temporarily dismantled; the prostitutes who fall victim to consumption and venereal disease, are seen going through their periodic routine medical examinations at local hospitals, ostensibly to protect them from syphilis. Yet it was not uncommon that the use of unsanitary instruments by the medical officials caused the transmission of the infections they were supposed to prevent.

The opening scene of *Camino del sur*, based on a story by Bedia Feijó and by Juan B. Stagnaro, focuses on the Jewish ritual slaughter of animals in a Polish *shtetl*. The first section—one of four which divide the film—is entitled "The Remount" which means, literally, "a fresh horse to replace one no longer available". The term derives from a chapter from Albert Londres' 1923 documentary book *Le Chemin de Buenos Aires* (The Road to Buenos Ayres (sic), already referred to in detail in chapter 1). "The remount" as a metaphor used by the human flesh slavers, stands for the cargos of girls who were taken away from their East European villages, shipped to Buenos Aires, and forced to practice prostitution.

Camino del sur follows step by step the "education" of a prostitute. It is incongruous in this case that the language spoken among the Jewish characters in a small Polish village is Polish, when in reality, the Jewish peasants spoke Yiddish while Polish was the language confined to the cities. When the setting moves to Buenos Aires, the languages spoken shift between Polish and Spanish. The religious life of the *shtetl* is recreated through wedding music and songs. The music evokes the landscape of the villages and the customs of a people that was annihilated during the second world war. In this film, however the melodies heard are in Polish and not in Yiddish. *Klezmer* music was customarily used for Jewish weddings in all the Eastern European countries. The traditional peasant head-scarves that the women wear here—decorated in front, and completely wrapped around the women's heads—also differ from the typically Jewish head-scarves.—The influence of the Jewish religion is perceived in the submissive behavior of the girls who did not object to the choices their parent made on their behalf. The film points to the compliance of the naive parents who were enticed by local procurers in the service of the traffickers, and innocently traded their unmarried girls for material convenience and for a future in Buenos Aires.

Such is the case in *Camino del sur*, which traces the itinerary of a young Polish man posing as a rich bridegroom who returns to Poland to find himself a wife and take her to Buenos Aires. After a Jewish religious ceremony, the newly-wed couple sets off to Argentina. The voyage across the Atlantic ocean becomes a prison for the young bride. The ship, as the place for their initiation in prostitution, provides the first setting for the imprisoned women to establish a relationship with other women in the same predicament. As Albert Londres explains in his account, it was common practice to treat the girls badly on the ship, and then offer them better conditions at the brothel.

The film briefly illustrates the influence of the *Zwi Migdal* organization. After the protagonist bears a child from the pimp who exploits her, he assures himself that she will never run away, by using their child as his weapon. He implies that even if he wanted to, he could not betray the *Zwi Migdal* for fear of his own life.

Camino del sur carefully depicts the *polaca's* life of torture, and her frequent attempts to escape. Her romantic, silent affair with a mysterious client at the brothel is one of several sub-plots that the film examines. The silence of the church and other institutions in an atmosphere of hypocrisy and double standards is symbolized in the *polaca's* trust in a client who seems to understand her when he sleeps with her, but who abandons her when she discovers he is a priest. Neither the Catholic priest—committed to celibacy—nor the prostitute—committed to selling herself to her clients—can express their intimate feelings openly.

Camino del sur also explores incestuous and homosexual relationships among the *polacas*. While still in Poland, as a young girl, the protagonist innocently flirts with her orthodox brother, enticing him to dance with her. For his part, the brother's faith and his secret attraction for his sister make him sexually repressed.

Within the frame of Carnival days, during which people walk the streets in disguise and allow themselves liberties they would not take during the rest of the year, the brother, much like a seventeenth century Spanish nobleman, comes to Buenos Aires to cleanse his family's honor. The tragic circle is closed at the end of the movie when the brother avenges his sister and ritually slaughters the pimp who was responsible for her disgrace. In the process, he is brutally murdered by the pimp's bodyguards.

(*Naked Tango*) *Tango desnudo* directed by Leonard Shrader, has an international cast which includes Fernando Rey from Spain, and Cipe Lincovsky from Argentina. A few glimpses of Rudolf Valentino—holding a whip in his hand and flaunting sharp spurs in his boots—set the tone of sex and violence for the rest of the film. In it, Valentino is seen challenging a rival and killing him before leading a woman in a tango. The dance introduces a series of tortuous sexual practices to which the victimized woman is submitted. From the voluminous body of literature derived from the tango, the observations made by the Argentine essayist Ezequiel Martínez Estrada seem most pertinent to its portrayal in *Naked Tango*. Martínez Estrada writes that although the tango initiated sexual encounters where men were supposed to be the dominant party, the dance itself did not signify male strength, but it reflected, instead, man's weakness. To him the dance was devoid of sensuality, since it had "the seriousness of the man during copulation because it seems to inseminate without pleasure."[32] Furthermore, Martínez Estrada proclaims that the tango humiliated women not because it demonstrated their sexual subordination, but rather because they were dominated by men as "passive" and as "bound" as themselves.

Naked Tango, a melodramatic thriller based on mistaken identities, opens during a transatlantic voyage from Europe to Argentina. Stephanie, a newly married woman, dissatisfied with her husband, seizes the opportunity to get away from her wealthy but old husband by taking the place of another woman—Alba—who has thrown herself overboard. Stephanie soon discovers that her new fate is worse than her worst nightmare. She falls into the claws of the white slavers who believe she is Alba, the *polaca* who had committed suicide.

During the decade of the 1920s Buenos Aires had gained a terrible international reputation as a sinful "tango" metropolis, and as a port where kidnapped European virgins unwillingly sold their bodies to strangers. Some of the stories came from those victims who escaped from sexual bondage and later told horrendous stories of seduction and brutality. Such is the case in this film, which follows the diary that Stephanie continues writing after Alba's death. In it she recounts how her husband "by proxy" picks her up her at the port of Buenos Aires and takes her to a house where her future mother-in-law gives her instructions on how to be a good Jewish wife.

In the role of the Polish madam, actress Cipe Lincovsky plays a character that evinces both curiosity and disgust. As the dutiful mother-in-law, she welcomes the bride with the background music of "A Yiddishe Mame" and a table full of food. To add to the cynicism of her part, she pretends to "understand" the bride by providing her with a chicken heart with which to stain the sheets during her nuptial night, to prove that she is a virgin, even if she is not.

Shrader only offers a glimpse of the behavior of the Jewish community, as it interrupts the wedding ceremony by creating a disturbance outside the synagogue. The bridegroom appeases his future wife by telling her: "Pay no attention to them. They are from a radical synagogue . . . They are jealous, I told you. There are no women in this city." The crowd is in fact demonstrating against the fake marriage performed by the impure faction of the community, the *Zwi Migdal*.

All throughout, there is an understanding between the government officials and the pimps, that makes the latter feel they own the city. When Alba runs away from the brothel and seeks help, the policemen are well acquainted with Rico Bornstein, the pimp who enslaved her. One of the officers remarks that "He says his wives are virgins from

Paris, but they are always Jews from Warsaw." And still, instead of saving the victim, they promptly deliver her back to her fake "husband" and to continued subjugation.

The Bornstein gang is set in competition with that of the *Zwi Migdal*, although, in the eyes of the Argentine gentiles, all the traffickers are part of the same maffia. The director offers just a glimpse of an auction of *polacas*, but enough to show how the pimps examine the "products" on display on a pedestal, and make remarks in Yiddish: "Gib a kook, a tooches, azah sheyne meydl" (Look at her buttocks, such a lovely girl).

It is significant that in *Naked Tango*, as in *Camino del sur,* the most powerful pimps turn out to be impotent men. Paradoxically, the film's most accomplished fantasy is that of the pimp who has everything at his disposal, but is sexually repressed. In *Naked Tango* the pimp fulfills his sexual fantasies through voyeurism, as he watches his own brother rape the enslaved woman he could have possessed. His only source of pleasure is to dance erotic tangos, not at a dancing hall, but at a slaughterhouse, sliding in pools of animal blood while holding an open jack-knife to his partner's throat.

Most readers acquainted with Esteban Echeverría's masterful 19th century story *El matadero (The Slaughterhouse),* will immediately recognize the situation depicted in that story and its parallel symbolism intended in this movie. Echeverría was condemning the ruthless measures taken by dictator Juan Manuel de Rosas against those who opposed his despotic ideas. The brutality seen at the siaughterhouse and the abuses of victims—women, foreigners—is clearly established in this film.

After attempting repeated flights from her exploiters, Alba succeeds in finding her legitimate husband. He recognizes her and reclaims her. Although for a while she returns to her life as the wife of a rich politician, her recent past interferes and the final tragedy cannot be averted. The pimp who claims her, follows and murders both her and her husband at the cost of his own life.

Under the direction of Jonathan Demme, *Last Embrace* is a thriller based on a novel by Murray Teigh Bloom—*The Thirteenth Man*—and on a screenplay by David Shaber. The action takes place in the 1970's, at colorfully selected sites in the United States, which include Niagara Falls and Princeton University. The heroine is a graduate student whose research leads her to discover the truth about her grandmother—a Polish immigrant—and to seek revenge for the tragedy that destroyed her health. She will now speak on her grandmother's behalf, and become her avenger. For that reason the director assigned the same actress to play both roles, that of grandmother and of granddaughter.

The plot relates only tangentially to the white slave trade, as it follows the track of a criminal organization of Jewish traffickers. Repeated murder attempts are made against the life of Harry Hannan (Roy Sheider), a government agent. Although there is no apparent relationship between himself and the other men murdered under strange circumstances, Hannan determines that they were Jewish. In the process of his investigation he also deciphers a first century A.D. code in Arameic from Deuteronomy, chapter XIX, verse 12. The words: "Goel Hadam", meaning "The Avenger of the Blood" only make sense to Hannan when he relates them to the other attempts which resulted in murder.

He finally discovers that the initials *Z.M.* stand for *Zwi Migdal*, the criminal organization that had its headquarters hidden behind an old synagogue located in the Lower East Side of New York. He finds the same initials scratched on his father's grave, and once again at the desk of a Princeton professor of anthropology. The serial murderer turns out to be a young woman (Janet Margolin) who pretended to be conducting scholarly research, when in fact she was tracking down the traffickers from the *Zwi Migdal* who were responsible for raping and prostituting her grandmother. Eva—who bears the same name as her grandmother—is committed to hunting and murdering the grandsons of those who wronged her grandmother.

It is only here and not in the other three films that the oppressed victim expresses her rage. It takes two generations after the events have taken place for a woman to avenge the crime. The granddaughter eloquently defends her grandmother's innocence and condemns men for turning her into a victim. That is why, although the granddaughter is tragically killed at the end of the chase, the spectators identify with her zeal for justice "vigilante style" and with her hopeless wish to redeem her grandmother's death.

For the first time, three generations removed from the dramatic events, a woman speaks about the rage and humiliation felt by the oppressed. Her crazy plot, in retribution for the actions committed against her grandmother, broke her body and spirit. As the Israeli novelist Aaron Appelfeld reflects when he observes the behavior of the grandchildren of Holocaust survivors, it took three generations for the victims to express their feelings of pain. They finally did it through their grandchildren. As they themselves were too shattered to speak about the brutalities they had suffered, and as their sons and daughters respected their silence, their children became their voice and cried out in their behalf.

NOTES

1. Shalom Asch, *God of Vengeance.* Boston, 1918 ed.

2. Shalom Asch, *Mottke the Thief,* New York, Putnam and Sons, 1935.

3. Leib Malach, *Ibergus,* Buenos Aires, 1923.

4. Leib Malach, *Don Domingo's Crossroads* Ed. B. Kletzkin, Editorial Vilna, Poland, 1930; and E.L. Peretz Publishing House, Israel. Fragments of this novel, translated into English by Nora Glickman and Rosalía Rosembuj appear in *Modern Jewish Studies,* New York, Queens College Publications, 1989, 17-32.

5. *Regeneraciíon.* Translation of Leib Malach's play *Ibergus* from the Yiddish into Spanish by Rosalía Rosembuj and Nora Glickman. Preliminary study by Nora Glickman, "La trata de blancas." Buenos Aires: Editorial Pardés, 1984.

6. *Leib Malach, vida y obra.* Edited by the Comité del Libro "Leib Malach", Los Angeles, 1949. (Copywright Lotty Malach).

7. Yaacov Botoshansky, "Some memories about *Ibergus:*To Leib Malach, in memoriam" *Di Presse,* 1936.

8. Leib Malach, "Letter from abroad: Two generations" *The Menorah Journal* 12-24; 408-416.

9. Jacobo Botoshansky, "Algunos recuerdos sobre *Ibergus.*" Buenos Aires: (entro de Artistas Judíos, 28–6–1926).

10. Melech Ravitch, "Jewish Criticism on Leib Malach: *Don Domingo's Crossroads*: A Novel of Great Reach" in *Leib Malach: Work and Life,* Ed. Lotty F. Malach, Los Angeles, 1949.

11. Isaac Bashevis Singer, "The Colony," *A Friend of Kafka and Other Stories.* New York: Farrar, Straus & Giroux, 1970.

12. Isaac Bashevis Singer, "Hanka," *Passions.* Greewich: Fawcet Books, 1951.

13. Part of the material from this section derives from my study entitled "The Jewish White Slave Trade in Latin American Writings," *American Jewish Archives: New Perspectives on Latin American Jewry.* Ed. by Judith Laikin Elkin, Nov. 1982, 178-189.

14. *Viento que lleva y trae.* Describes a brothel in Isla Maciel, next to Buenos Aires.

15. Alberto Novión, *El cambalache de Petroff,* Revista Teatral "Nuestro Teatro," Buenos Aires, April 1937.

16. Julián Martel, *La bolsa,* Buenos Aires, Editorial Huemul, S.A., 1957.

17. Donna Guy, *Sex and Danger in Buenos Aires* Lincoln: University of Nebraska Press, 1991.

18. Manuel Gálvez, *Nacha Regules,* Buenos Aires: Centro Editor de América Latina, 1968.

19. Samuel Eichelbaum, *Nadie la conoció nunca,* Buenos Aires: Ediciones del Carro de Tespis, 1956.

20. David Viñas *En la Semana Trágica,* Buenos Aires: José Alvares, 1966.

21. David Viñas, *Los dueños de la tierra,* Buenos Aires: Editorial Librería Lorraine, 1974.

22. Alicia Muñoz, *Las crónicas de Pichincha,* Buenos Aires, n.d.

23. Reissued *Versos de una . . .* (with an extensive critical study by Isabel Irizarry). Buenos Aries: Editorial Rescate, 1977.

24. Clara Béter (pseudonym of César Tiempo) *Verses of a . . .* Buenos Aires: Editorial Rescate, 1926.

25. Elías Castelnuovo (pseud. Ronald Chaves) in *Versos de una . . .* Buenos Aires: Claridad, n.d. pp. 12-13.

26. Leonardo Senkman, *La identidad judía en la literatura argentina* Buenos Aires: Pardés, 1983, 169-172.

27. César Tiempo, *Clara Béter y otras fatamorganas* Buenos Aires: Peña Lillo, 1974, 17-24.

28. David Viñas, *Pluralismo e identidad: lo judío en la literatura argentina.* Buenos Aires: Milá 1986, 50-52.

29. Mario Szichman, *A las 20:25 la señora entró en la inmortalidad,* Hanover, Ediciones del Norte, 1981.

30. Israel Chas de Cruz, *Aventuras de la picaresca porteña,* Buenos Aires, Editorial Freeland, 1966, 17-21.

31. Moacyr Scliar, *O ciclo das águas,* Porto Alegre, Editora Globo, 1978.

32. Ezequiel Martínez Estrada, *Radiografía de la Pampa.* Buenos Aires: Babel, 1933.

CHAPTER III

Raquel Liberman

Raquel . . .
Her fate was that of a bird
that sings only in Spring
Raquel . . .
Her fate was that of a plant
that only grows in solitude.
You were woman, bird, tree,
wail, trill, courage.
Woman of a wild flight
that could never fly.
Cry of a thrush—oh, so bitter—
that could never sing,
bud of sun and ivy,
ivy of sun that grows
without a wall to climb.

But one day . . .
Raquel of many days,
you were that bird that took to flight.
Fly, Raquel,
as mirrors and doors and winds
await you!
Your thoughts are mirrors,
your open hand is the door
and your winds that never cease
to dream . . . to dream.

Your song, a mast in the wind
that sails in freedom.
Open your mirror door,
ask the sun for a reflection
that lights up your truth,
Raquel of the walls and the ivy,
give me a piece of mirror, woman-bird
Give me a mirror heart,
inlaid with voice . . .
your wicker voice that sings:
I AM FREE! . . .
                    I AM FREE!

Carlos Luis Serrano
Raquel Liberman: A story from Pichincha

It is always a challenge to write the faithful biography of a person when the myth about him or her has already taken flight, and when popular imagination has taken care of augmenting and even improving the historical facts. Various considerations then emerge. On the one hand, the writer has to become a thorough critic of the information backed by documentation, and reveal the accomplishments as well as the failures of the life it refers to. On the other hand, it has to welcome with enthusiasm the legends and speculations about its protagonist.

It becomes clear, upon close examination of Raquel's letters (the only legacy available today in her own hand-writing) along with the photos of herself and her family, and with the documents gathered in this book, that Raquel deliberately chose to lead a double life, and to tell the public only part of the truth about herself. We are moved to review a period she chose to keep in obscurity and to appreciate how wrenching her life must have been during the years as a prostitute between 1924 and 1928. These years were followed by her rebellion against the system that enslaved her. Her personal liberation meant the beginning of a successful campaign against the traffickers' organization. If what came earlier might add an original and surprising dimension to Raquel's life, if we view it as the experience of an incoming immigrant from Poland to South America, Raquel's biography is similar to that of many other women with families. The difference lies in the circumstances that forced her to change her course.

I. RAQUEL LIBERMAN: THE HISTORICAL VERSION

Up to the present we only had knowledge of Raquel Liberman exactly as she had portrayed herself publicly. In her identity card, taken in 1925, Raquel states that her marital status is "single." She declares to the police in 1929 that she arrived from Warsaw in Buenos Aires in 1924, accompanied by Bronya Coyman, and that the latter turned out to be an agent of the *Zwi Migdal.* Coyman was the auxiliary that led Raquel to her first exploiter, Jaime Cissinger. After four years as a prostitute in Buenos Aires, Raquel manages to pay for her freedom, opens an antique shop and becomes independent from the traffickers' bond. Her freedom, however is not real. She suffers from continuous pressure from the traffickers who steal her belongings and her jewelry. At this point Raquel issues her first denunciation in October 1929. Her marriage to Salomón Korn had been another trick by the Migdal to force her to return to prostitution. Raquel rejects the bribery and the threats that follow.[1]

Raquel fails to get Simón Brutkievich to intercede in her favor and help her get her money back from the *Zwi Migdal.* Supported by a representative of the *Ezrat Nashim* (Association for the Rehabilitation of Fallen Women) she appears on December 31, 1929, before Julio Alsogaray, the Commissar-Inspector of the federal police, acting for the second time as the informer against the *Zwi Migdal* association for crimes of corruption, extortion and blackmail.[2] Between 1926 and 1929 Alsogaray had been collecting incriminating documentation from other victims, and was now ready to act against the traffickers. Liberman's complaint was submitted to the prosecuting Judge Manuel Rodriguez Ocampo, who ordered a general investigation after he discovered that José Salomón Korn, the pimp who had "married" Raquel, had been exploiting other prostitutes, and that they were afraid to testify against him. Ocampo ordered mass arrests, the *Zwi Migdal* headquarters raided and the documents seized.

Throughout all her declarations Raquel shows her determination to keep her past from the authorities. We can only assume that her purpose was to keep to herself her years as a wife and a mother that, in spite of the deprivations, were the happiest years of her life. She remained silent about her adolescence, her marriage to Yaacov Ferber, the birth of her two sons, and her great illusions with respect to Argentina.

One can only speculate that if Raquel was so adamant to hide that aspect of her life, her deliberate effort towards anonymity was to protect the future of her children.

II. THE UNKNOWN RAQUEL:

Raquel Liberman was born in Berdichev, Kiev, on July 10, 1900.[3] She was not Polish by nationality, but Russian. She emigrated to Poland as a child, where the rest of her family lived. In Warsaw she met Yaacov Ferber, whom she married on December 21, 1919, with a full Jewish ceremony, including a "Ketubah"[4].

Both partners held occupations that allowed them to earn their living. Yaacov was a tailor, Raquel was a seamstress. In 1920 their first son, Sruga (Shaie) David Ferber, was born. In July 1921 Yaacov Ferber travelled to Argentina, where his sister Helke and her husband had been living for a few years. Yaacov's intention was to find work in Argentina and gather the necessary amount to send tickets to his family. In spite of the difficulties that arose from the separation, Raquel accepted this situation with resignation and optimism. When he arrived in Argentina, Yaacov Ferber joined his sister and brother-in-law who lived in the small village of Tapalqué, in the province of Buenos Aires. Here he soon did away with some of his Eastern European habits and clothing.

On October 22, 1922 Raquel disembarked in Buenos Aires with her two sons. She found that her husband was very frail in health, that he had no employment and was obliged to visit a hospital very frequently. Although it was never established from what ailment Yaacov suffered, it was probably tuberculosis, which was very common during those years.

After her arrival, Raquel and her children also established themselves in Tapalqué. Raquel's relations with her new relatives turned out to be no easier than with her relatives in Warsaw, since here just as much as there, she depended entirely on their help.

When the death of Raquel's husband occurred in 1923, a few months after she had emigrated to Argentina, Raquel became the sole support of her family. As a widow, aged 23, with two small children, and with poor knowledge of Spanish, Raquel found little chance to earn a living in her provincial village. As she could not leave her children with her relatives (her sister-in-law Helke was childless, and she was an invalid) Raquel entrusted them to a neighbor couple with children, and she left for Buenos Aires all alone. Raquel expected that, as she had stressed to Yaacov in one of her letters, being a seamstress would serve her well in Buenos Aires. Within the Jewish community she intended to meet traders with whom she could speak Yiddish until she learned the language. Apparently Raquel did not know of the fate of thousands of women that arrived alone in Buenos Aires. Unless they were being expected by relatives or people who knew them, these women were in danger of being kidnapped by madams or by traffickers and taken to the brothels. The corruption went so far that the *Ezrat Nashim*—an organization with a central office in London that had representatives in Rio de Janeiro, Montevideo and Buenos Aires—sent their agents to Argentina for the purpose of warning the naive women before they got off the boats, and putting them in the hands of responsible relatives.

We do not know the precise circumstances that led Raquel Liberman to seek employment in prostitution. One may speculate that she went into that profession in desperation, in order to help her children. Unlike other women exploited by traffickers, Raquel did not depend on her *caftan* Jaime Cissinger. She was allowed the "grace" of paying him a percentage of her earnings in exchange for his protection. As soon as she could put away enough money to buy her own freedom, Raquel did not hesitate to abandon "the life". For that purpose she enlisted the help of another compatriot who kept the money for her rescue. She also put away her identity card certifying she was a prostitute and, with the money she had saved, she started an antique business on Callao street. Somewhat later she married José Salomón Korn—nicknamed the Bolshevik—at the synagogue in Córdoba street. Raquel still did not know that the synagogue was the central office of the *Zwi Migdal* and never suspected that her marriage was a farce.

The honeymoon turned out to be very short, since Raquel soon found out that her husband was a trafficker who had been sent expressly by the *Zwi Migdal*. Besides taking away her belongings, Korn forced his "wife" to resettle in the brothel at Valentín Gómez' street, in Buenos Aires.

The police investigation verifies that, apart from stealing 90,000.00 pesos from Raquel Liberman, Korn exploited other wards. When Raquel asked Simón Brutkievich to intercede in her favor and help her get her money back, she did not know that he was the president of the *Zwi Migdal*. Brutkievich proposed to compensate her by returning just a part of the money and the jewels they had stolen, as long as she withdrew her complaint to the police. But rather than surrender or give in, Raquel stayed firm in her action. In response, Brutkievich first assigned one of his followers—Mauricio Kirstein—to threaten her physically. He also sent José S. Korn to make her a formal marriage proposal.

This was the opportunity that police Inspector Julio Alsogaray had been waiting for years: to take action against the criminal organization of the *Zwi Migdal*, and to provide all detailed information to Judge Manuel Rodriguez Ocampo. Although it may seem inconceivable, following the terrible experiences Raquel lived through during her first years in the brothel, she became again a victim of the traffickers. And yet, once she had established herself at her antique shop, it was natural that she should chose to share the rest of her life with a man who understood her. This was, however, the way in which Raquel once more became subservient and how she was disposessed of all of her belongings. Having failed in her attempts to gain her freedom, Raquel Liberman registered on January 1930 at the Police station to go back into prostitution.

When the syndicate of procurers sent Raquel Liberman's and José S. Korn's papers to the court, they presented the latter as a victim, while Raquel was described as a prostitute by profession. They declared that she was[5] living a double life, "given to prostitution in her country of origin," and that

> she continued practicing it since her arrival in Buenos Aires without interrupting the obligatory visits to the Municipal Health Office when she set up her business. In this manner she would not lose the authorization to go back to prostitution.

Furthermore, the investigators in charge found proof that the multiple commercial activities of Mr. José Salomón Korn were indisputably honorable. In consequence, Raquel endured two more months of slavery before she managed to appear again in front of Judge Rodriguez Ocampo, and put her fate and that of her sons entirely in his hands.

To what extent was her feat unique? It is well documented that there were other slaves who dared to act in their own defense, yet failed in their intent.[6] The valor of Raquel resides in her determination to carry out her mission of justice and to persevere until she was victorious. It is thanks to her that the newspapers published detailed lists with the names of the traffickers and of the "regents" that operated the *Zwi Migdal.*

Out of the 434 active members who were called to appear in front of Judge Manuel Rodriguez Ocampo, only 108 were convicted of delinquency. The sentences of the Judicial Process were not sufficiently severe. Several Buenos Aires' newspapers demanded that the governmental provisional government should deport the traffickers.

As a result of Raquel's denunciation and of the campaign mounted by the Jewish community and by the Association for the Protection of Girls and Women, dozens of brothels were closed up and most pimps were jailed or deported. The lawyers of the traffickers called it blackmail against the *Zwi Migdal*; they helped more than a hundred of the accused men to flee the country, and they put up multiple obstacles for Judge Rodriguez Ocampo who functioned as prosecutor in Argentine law. Ocampo ordered a general investigation of the Liberman case.[7] Between 1926 and 1929 in spite of all the ruses conceived by the traffickers, Alsogaray uncovered several criminal cases, including those of Ita Kaiser from Warsaw, who was twenty years old when rescued; of Bonny Spigler, who was found gravely ill from being locked up in a brothel; and of Perla Pezzeborska, a woman who threw a note from the window, hoping to be saved from her fate. Alsogaray's actions contributed to drastically curtailing the organized white slave market in Argentina.

By her public denunciation in 1928 Raquel Liberman became a symbol. More than a symbol, she became a myth. Her action represents not only the struggle of the enslaved woman to obtain her own freedom, but the struggle of the victims against the maffia of exploiters.

Paradoxically, Raquel succeeded in concealing her family life throughout her years with the *Zwi Migdal.* She kept secret her legal marriage in Poland, and the birth of her children in order to protect their future. The persona she showed the public was that of a woman who arrived alone to Buenos Aires, and who was forced into prostitution.

In 1934, Raquel Liberman applied for a visa to return to Poland to visit her family. The IWO (Jewish Scientific Institute)sent a letter to the

Polish Consulate in Buenos Aires, providing information regarding the moral conduct and means of survival "of a certain Raquel Liberman." Such a request was commonplace during those years, due to the scandals resulting from the dealings of the *Zwi Migdal*. The intention of the Polish government was to seek proof that Raquel Liberman had nothing to do with that organization anymore.[8]

The voyage to Poland never took place, since only a few months later, when Raquel was just 35 years old, she was admitted into Argerich hospital, where she died of thyroid cancer on April 7, 1935.

Half a century after Raquel Liberman's death, the puzzle of her private life can be completed thanks to the letters, documents and photographs provided by her grandchildren. It is worth pointing out that today, sixty years later, the public is also more tolerant and better prepared to understand what took place during the plight of this desperate woman.

In a couple of interviews I conducted with Raquel's grandchildren, both tell anecdotes and memories of their father, that serve to better comprehend the psychological impact Raquel's actions had on her children and grandchildren.[9] Shaie David, Raquel's older son, loved to sing. When he was still an adolescent, he prepared himself for a singing contest and won the first prize. When he went to pick it up, however, he was asked to show his identification papers. Young Ferber chose not to receive his prize, which involved declaring his nationality, since, in his mind, to have been born in Poland was enough to establish a connection between him and the prostitution ring.

Raquel's grandchildren also relate that unlike the majority of Jewish immigrants who insisted that only their male sons had to complete their studies, Josué D. Farber—Raquel's older son—insisted that his daughter should have a profession that would assure her independence and means of subsistence. Consequently, he made sure that his children—particularly his daughter—were brought up with strict supervision. He forbade his daughter to go out alone, even when she had a formal boyfriend. Fearing, perhaps, that her daughter's life was in danger, the father constantly warned her against the danger of strangers.

In his commentary on the impact of the Holocaust on the children of survivors, the Israeli novelist Aaron Appelfeld observes that many memories were deliberately destroyed by those who suffered torture and humiliation in concentration camps.[10]

> Their subsequent life demanded the destruction of painful memories. For the survivors, the present was to them the most beautiful, splendorous time, while the past, with all its pain and horror emerged as a fine shell, like an illusion, under which it panted like a wounded animal. They fought against the past by denying it, by hiding it. They did everything possible to be themselves, they adapted to the new milieu and became like everyone else, to assure themselves that what they had suffered was hidden in an abyss. Their desire to conceal, forget and change was more powerful than any other. So they revealed nothing to their own children, who grew up in a void.
>
> But not many years after their parents' rehabilitation, the voices of their children and grandchildren attempted to find out what happened so many years ago. Why did their grandparents keep quiet, why were they mute? Those children are now revealing what their parents had failed to disclose. Those far-away, recondite memories imprisoned for years have rolled on to the grandchildren and are now resurging and renewing the literature written on this subject. The years of denial have left their imprint. (32)

In Raquel Liberman's case, her children did not succeed in freeing themselves of their mother's shady past. The suffering of so many years had shamed them to the point of silence. But her grandchildren are the faithful voices of their grandmother's plight, and they are now beginning to talk with clarity. One should hope that soon the literature written on this subject will be radically modified.

As a consequence of such upbringing, Raquel Liberman's grandchildren grew up believing that curiosity of any sort can be dangerous. Although they knew none of the details of their grandmother's life, they lived in fear of disclosure. When they discovered their grandparents' letters, photographes and documents, they came to realize that Raquel Liberman deserved to be vindicated in the history of immigrant women, and understood as a wife and mother who provided for the sustenance of her family.

RAQUEL LIBERMAN IN FICTION:

Basing himself on the historical accounts available to him in the 1970s, Humberto Costantini created a "Rapsodia de Raquel Liberman," (Rapsody of Raquel Liberman) which is a fictional biography of Raquel, a woman whose terrible humiliation as a prostitute drove her to disobedience and rebellion. Costantini describes Raquel's virtual imprisonment in a Buenos Aires brothel. Overcome by sudden death in 1987, Costantini left his "Rapsodia de Raquel Liberman" unedited, a novel about the woman who "accepted her real embattled destiny by facing the mighty.[11]

Shortly before his death Costantini composed a series of poems to the memory of Raquel Liberman. In his "Milonga de una mujer" (Milonga of a woman) (1987) he praises her courage in confronting the *Zwi Migdal*. Costantini admires the woman who resisted "la coima y el canfinflero polaco" (the bribes and the Polish pimp), who spent ten years in a "casa mala" (house of ill repute) taking the beatings of her traffickers, and who found her only consolation in old Yiddish songs that reminded her of her past life in the Polish *shtetl*. More than a "milonga"—a sad tango-like ballad—his nostalgic verses are an anthem to dignity.

The play by Carlos Luis Serrano, *Raquel, Liberman una historia de Pichincha*, (1992), that opened in Rosario in 1988, puts Raquel Liberman on a pedestal.[12] Although it corroborates in part the historical facts surrounding the Liberman case, Serrano's version also moves away from reality as it presents the protagonist as a poor, innocent woman who was sold to the traffickers in her Polish village. The end of the play is melodramatic: Serrano's Raquel sacrifices herself only in order to prevent the traffickers from killing her friend Sara, who had been tortured for having intended to flee from the claws of her kidnappers. When Raquel discovers that Sara has succumbed to torture, Raquel has nothing else to lose, and makes her denunciation public. Serrano's production uses the Carnival festivities to represent the cabaret background that dominates his entire dramatization of Raquel Liberman's life.

In her televised mini-series *Te llamarás Raquel* (You Will Be Named Raquel; 1993), Myrta Shalom speculates about the psychological motivations of the heroine, Raquel Liberman.[13] This eight-hour version recreates a story of love, uprootedness and hope.

The young *polaca* is deceived by Zwi, "rufián en el prostíbulo y señor en la casa."(a trafficker at the brothel and a lord at home),[14] Zwi is married to a decent and submissive wife. His son is a journalist who risks his life to his relentless desire to divulge the infamous traffic of women. Myrta Shalom portrays a world of rivalries among the women of the brothel. Raquel's native language, Yiddish, is used here to incorporate sentimental elements, such as childhood songs. It also serves to separate the sophisticated Jewish-European world from the vulgar expressions in Spanish employed by the members of the brothel.

Like José Serrano in his play, Shalom draws on the historical data based on the Liberman case. To complement her fiction she dramatizes Raquel Liberman's denunciation of the traffic to the police authorities with the help of the Chief of Police Julio Alsogaray and of Judge Manuel R. Ocampo. In her fictionalization of a love-affair between the head of the *Zwi Migdal*—a "respectable" Jewish family man, and a furrier by profession—and Raquel Liberman, the latter is depicted as totally innocent and easily deceived by her pimp.

Finally, my own dramatization *Una tal Raquel* (*A Certain Raquel*; 1993) is based on the letters, photos and documents that were made available to me by Raquel Liberman's grandchildren.[15] When analyzed individually, these materials disclose important aspects of Raquel Liberman, which force us to interpret the rest of her life from a different perspective. The technical device used in my play involves a conversation between Raquel Liberman's granddaughter—seeking to uncover her grandmother's mystery—and Raquel herself. *A Certain Raquel* is a *collage* composed of documentary and anecdotal material. It also contains fragments of the literature related to Jewish white slavery and to Argentine immigration. Scenes from Leib Malach's *Ibergus* compose this play within the play, which present to modern audiences the theater experience during the 1930s and provide a window into Raquel Liberman's contemporary audience. The play skips the chronological order by confronting Raquel Liberman, age thirty five, with her granddaughter—the same age as Raquel. Put thus into perspective, and with the help of Raquel Liberman's actual letters and photographs, the audiences can better appreciate the sacrifices and the hard decisions Raquel had to make on her way from bondage to freedom. Her unspoken life is now taken up by her granddaughter.

NOTES

1. *Crítica,* Buenos Aires, May 23, 1930.

2. Julio Alsogaray, *Trilogía de la trata de blancas: Rufianes. Policía. Municipalidad.* Buenos Aires, Editorial Tor, 1933.

3. All the original documents and letters used here are unpublished Permission to reproduce them was given by Raquel and Horacio Ferber, Raquel Liberman's grandchildren..

4. *Ketubbah,* (Heb. "writ"): An Arameic document containing a staement of the obligations which the bridegroom undertakes toward his bride and which in rabbinic law is a prerequisite of marriage *The Encyclopedia of Jewish Religion.* Jerusalem: Massada Press Ltd., 1967, 226.

5. Goldar as much as Alsogaray devote long pages to expose the tricks used by the traffickers and their lawyers in order to obstruct the course of Justice.

6. Names of victims and places where it was published.

7. Edward Bristow, *Prostitution and Prejudice*, New York:Schoken Books, 1986.

8. The Partial text from this letter was found in the archives of the YIVO in Buenos Aires.

9. Interview with Rosalía Rosembuj, by Nora Glickman.

10. Aarón Appelfeld, *Diálogo*, Jerusalem, Spring 1994, 32.

11. Humberto Costantini. *Rapsodia de Raquel Liberman* (fragments) *Cien años de narrativa judeo-argentina.* Milá, Buenos Aires, 1989, 194–202.

12. Carlos Luis Serrano, *Teatro: Raquel Liberman, una historia de Pichincha.* Rosario, Editorial Ross, 1927.

13. Myrta Shalom, *Te llamarás Raquel*, Buenos Aires, in 1992, unpublished.

14. Nora Glickman, *Una tal Raquel*, unpublished version.

CHAPTER IV

Documentation

DOCUMENTATION ON RAQUEL LIBERMAN:

1. Raquel Liberman's certificate of attendance to "Jerusalem", a Jewish school in Warsaw. August 3, 1910.
2. 1919. *Ketuba*, (Official religious matrimonial contract) Lodz, Poland.
3. Sep. 20, 1920. Birth certificate of Raquel's first son, Sruga (David) Ferber.
4. August 24, 1922. Polish passport of Raquel and her two children stamped by the Argentine Consulate in Warsaw.
5. Health certificate issued to Raquel in Warsaw, September 1, 1922.
6. Working permit issued for Raquel (as a seamstress), September 1, 1922.
7. Raquel's good behavior certificate.
8. Boarding certificate issued to Raquel by the Argentine Consulate in Warsaw, September 1, 1922.
9. Raquel Liberman's identification card, July 11, 1922. restamped in Cherbourg, 1922.
10. Letter from the IWO (Jewish Scientific Institute) to the Polish Consulate in Buenos Aires in answer to a request for information regarding "the moral conduct and the means of subsistence of a certain Raquel Liberman".
11. Translation of IWO's letter.
12. Death certificate for Raquel Liberman, Argerich Hospital, Buenos Aires, April 7, 1935.

1. Raquel Liberman's certificate of attendence to "Jerusalem", a Jewish school in Warsaw, August 3, 1910.

למזל טוב

יַעֲלֶה וְיָבֹא כְּגַן רָטֹב   וַיֹּאמֶר לִדְבַק טוֹב
וִיפַק רָצוֹן מֵהָאֵל הַטּוֹב   מָצָא אִשָּׁה מָצָא טוֹב

הַמַּגִּיד בֵּרֵאשִׁית אַחֲרִית, הוּא יִתֵּן שֵׁם טוֹב וּשְׁאֵרִית, לְאֵלֶּה דִּבְרֵי הַתְּנָאִים וְהַהַבְרִית שֶׁנִּדְבְּרוּ וְהִתְנוּ בֵּין בְּנֵי הַבְּרִי...

הַצְּדָדִים, לָטֵינָא מִצַּד הֶחָתָן הרב _____

הֶעָסוֹק מִצַּד _____

וּמִצַד הַשֵּׁנִי הֶה _____

הֶעָסוֹק מִצַּד _____ וּבִשְׁאֵלַת פִּיו וְאֶמְרָה הֵן.

ר"ד הֵה הֶחָתָן _____ תליל. יֵלֵךְ לְמַזָּל טוֹב וּבְשָׁעָה מוּצְלַחַת

אֶת הַכַּלָּה _____ תליל. בְּחוּפָּה וְקִדּוּשִׁין כְּדָת מֹשֶׁה וְיִשְׂרָאֵל.

וְאַל יַבְרִיחוּ וְאַל יַעֲלִימוּ לֹא זֶה מִזֶּה, וְלֹא זֶה מִזֶּה שׁוּם שַׁוֶּה הַבְרָחַת מָמוֹן בְּעוֹלָם, רַק יִשְׁלְטוּ בְּנִכְסֵיהֶן שָׁוֶה בְּשָׁוֶה .

וְיָדוּרוּ בְּאַהֲבָה וּבְחִבָּה כְּאוֹרַח כָּל אַרְעָא .

הֵה _____ תליל, הֶעָסוֹק מִצַּד _____ תליל. הַמְחֻיָּב אֶת עַצְמוֹ לְמַּר

הִתְחַיֵּב גַּם כֵּן לְהַלְבִּישׁ וּלְהַנְעִיל אֶת הֶחָתָן תליל קֹדֶם הַחֲתוּנָה בִּגְדֵי חוֹל וְשַׁבָּת וְיוֹם טוֹב בְּנָתָן, פֶּרֶים וְכַפָּתוֹת כְּנָתָן.

הֵה _____ תליל, הֶעָסוֹק מִצַּד _____ הִתְחַיֵּב אֶת עַצְמוֹ לִסְפָרִים נְדוּנְיָא אֵיזֶה

הִתְחַיֵּב גַּם כֵּן לְהַלְבִּישׁ וּלְהַנְעִיל אֶת הַכַּלָּה תליל קֹדֶם הַחֲתוּנָה תליל בִּגְדֵי חוֹל וְשַׁבָּת וְיוֹם טוֹב, פֶּרֶים וְכַפָּתוֹת וּטַ"ם וכ"פ

צְעִיפִים וְדַרְדִּיס הַכֹּל בְּנָתָן. הַחֲתוּנָה תִּהְיֶה לְמַזָּל טוֹב וּבְשָׁעָה מוּצְלַחַת אִם יִרְצֶה הַשֵּׁם _____

עַל הוֹצָאוֹת _____ וְתוֹךְ הַזְּמַן פָּסֵי שֶׁיֵּתְרַצוּ הַצְּדָדִים, רחו"ש וכל"י וּמֵרוּשִׁין לַחֲצָאִין.

קְנֶס מִצַּד הֶעָסוֹק לְצַד הַמַּכְנִיס חָצִי נָכוֹן, וְהַקְנֶס לֹא יְפַ... וכו', וּמַחֲמַת עֵידוּר וּקְטָטָה חַס וְשָׁלוֹם יִתְנַגֵּדוּ בְּקִנְקַנְת שִׁ...

עֶרֶב קִנְקַן מִצַּד הֶחָתָן _____ עֶרֶב קַבְּלָן מִצַּד הַכַּלָּה _____

הַצְּדָדִים מְחוּיָּבִים לַעֲשׂוֹת אֶת קָצָב שֶׁלֹּא יֵיעַ לָהֶם שׁוּם הֶזֵּק וְגֶרֶם הֶזֵּק ה... וְשָׁלוֹם מַחֲמַת הַעֲרוֹב קַבְּלָנוּת תליל.

וְקָנְיָנָא מְהַצְּדָדִים וְהֶחָתָן וּמְהַכַּלָּה עַל כָּל מַה דִּכְתוּב תליל עַל מַה דְּכָתוּב וּמְפֹרַשׁ לְעֵיל בְּכָלִי כָּשֵׁר לִסְבָנְיָא בֵּיה.

יוֹם ____ חֹדֶשׁ _____ שְׁנַת תר__ לפ"ק פֹּה _____

וְהַכֹּל שָׁרִיר וְקַיָּם.

וְנָאֻם _____ נָאֻם הָעֵדִים _____

וְיֶתֶר תּוּקֶף וְעוֹד מוֹהַר מַ"ייל בָּאוּ הַצְּדָדִים וְהֶחָתָן וְהַכַּלָּה תליל בְּעַצְמָם עַל הֶחָתוּם, יוֹם תר"ל שְׁנַת תל"ל.

נָאֻם _____ נָאֻם הֶחָתָן _____

נָאֻם _____ נָאֻם הַכַּלָּה _____

2. 1919. *Ketuba*, (Official religious matrimonial contract) Lodz, Poland.

בשבת _____ _____ _____ פלוני   שנת חמשת אלפים

ושש מאות _____ _____ לבריאת עולם למנין שאנו מנין כאן _____

איך _____ יצחק   בר _____ בן _____   אמר לה להדא

בתולתא _____   בת _____   הוי לי

לאנתו כדת משה וישראל ואנא אפלח ואוקיר ואיזון ואפרנס יתיכי ליכי

כהלכת גוברין יהודאין דפלחין ומוקירין וזנין ומפרנסין לנשיהון בקושטא

ויהיבנא ליכי מהר בתוליכי כסף זוזי מאתן דחזי ליכי מדאורייתא ומזוניכי

וכסותיכי וסיפוקיכי ומיעל לותיכי כאורח כל ארעא. וצביאת מרת _____

בתולתא דא והות ליה לאנתו. ודן נדוניא דהנעלת ליה מבי _____ בין בכסף

בין בדהב בין בתכשיטין במאני דלבושא בשימושי דירה ובשמושא דערסא

הכל קבל עליו ר' _____ — חתן דנן במאה זקוקים כסף

צרוף וצבי ר' _____ חתן דנן והוסיף לה מן דיליה עוד מאה זקוקים

כסף צרוף אחרים כנגדן. סך הכל מאתים זקוקים כסף צרוף וכך אמר ר'

_____ — חתן דנא אחריות שטר כתובתא דא נדוניא דן ותוספתא דא

קבלית עלי ועל ירתי בתראי להתפרע מכל _____ ספר ארג נכסין וקנינין דאית

תחות כל שמיא דקנאי ודעתיד אנא למקנא נכסין דאית להון אחריות ודלית

להון אחריות כלהון יהון אחראין וערבאן לפרוע מנהון שטר כתובתא דא

נדוניא דן ותוספתא דא מנאי ואפילו מן גלימא דעל כתפאי בחיי ובמותי מן

יומא דנן ולעלם. ואחריות שטר כתובתא דא נדוניא דן ותוספתא דא קבל עליו

ר' _____ — חתן דנן כחומר כל שטרי כתובות ותוספתא דנהגין

בבנת ישראל העשויין כתיקון חז"ל דלא כאסמכתא ודלא כטופסי דשטרי _____

מנ"ר _____ — בר _____ _____ חתן דנן

למרת _____ — בת _____ _____ בתולתא דא על כל

מה דכתוב ומפורש לעיל במנא דכשר למקניא ביה **והכל שריר וקים**

נאם _____ בן _____

ונאם _____ _____

2. *(continued.)*

3. Sep. 20, 1920. Birth certificate of Raquel's first son, Sruga (David) Ferber.

4. August 24, 1922. Polish passport of Raquel and her two children stamped by the Argentine Consulate in Warsaw.

4. August 24, 1922. Polish passport of Raquel and her two children stamped by the Argentine Consulate in Warsaw.

5. Health certificate issued to Raquel in Warsaw, September 1, 1922.

6. Working permit issued for Raquel (as a seamstress),
September 1, 1922.

7. Raquel's good behavior certificate.

8. Boarding certificate issued to Raquel by the Argentine Consulate in Warsaw, September 1, 1922.

9. Raquel Liberman's identification card, July 11, 1922. restamped in Cherbourg, 1922.

INSTITUTO CIENTIFICO JUDIO-IWO
PASTEUR 633 · 3°
1028 Bs. As.   ☎ 47-6624

se encuentra detenido, a la espera de ser embarcado en breve pla-
zo.-

Al privar a Gurlevich de su libertad, la mujer recu-
peró su libre albedrío, para dignificar su vida: en este momento
estamos preconizando la regeneración de la mujer en cuestión, a
la que prodigamos nuestros estímulos: Con los pequeños ahorros que
posee tiene la intención de abandonar el país para regresar a
Polonia, donde reside su madre y otros miembros de la familia.-

LIBERMAN, RUCHLA (RAQUEL).-

El nombre de Raquel Liberman es hartamente conocido
por la vinculación que había tenido al ventilarse el proceso
"Migdal" y, por lo tanto, no es necesario entrar en otras consi-
deraciones que las que nos interesa para el caso que vamos a
exponer.-

El Consulado de Polonia se ha dirigido a nuestra
Institución, solicitando establecer la situación moral y medios
de vida de una tal Raquel Liberman, la que requería un pasaporte
de viaje.- Ya lo hemos señalado en varias oportunidades que el
Consulado recurre, habitualmente a los servicios de nuestra ofi-
cina, a objeto de comprobar si los que tienen que embarcarse no
pertenecen al elemento tenebroso.-

Iniciadas las diligencias para identificar a la
nombrada mujer, se constató que se trataba de la Liberman, a
quién conocíamos a través del proceso "Migdal"; el pasado y an-
tecedentes de ella obraban en nuestro poder en todos sus detalle
pero nos interesaba averiguar su ocupación actual.-

Con el correr del tiempo había perdido de vida

10. Letter from the IWO (Jewish Scientific Institute) to the Polish Consulate in Buenos Aires in answer to a request for information regarding "the moral conduct and the means of subsistance of a certain Raquel Liberman."

INSTITUTO CIENTIFICO JUDIO
PASTEUR 633 - 3°
1028 Bs. As.   ☎ 47-6824

ignorabamos absolutamente lo que hacía ahora.-

Llevar la investigación en una forma discreta hubiera ofrecido el inconveniente de tener que distraer mucho tiempo, del que no disponemos, lo que nos indujo a visitar a la Liberman en su domicilio; conforme transpusimos el dintel de la puerta, la primera impresión que recibimos fué de nuestro agrado: cualquiera que la viera ahora en ese nuevo ambiente, que se intuía sano, estaría lejos de suponer que esa mujer se había entregado a una vida licenciosa por espacio de varios años. Y, sin embargo, el estigma deja, por lo general, un sello indeleble en los rostros de muchas de las que tuvieron la desgracia de entregarse continuamente a prácticas viciosas; la Liberman nos sugiere un concepto favorable, porque constituye un contraste bien grato, por cierto, con otras mujeres también redimidas, y las que en su nueva condición incitaron nuestro interés para observarlas de cerca.-

Abordada la cuestión que nos interesaba, la Liberman se mostró muy dispuesta a suministrarnos todos los datos que le fueron requeridos, a fin de poder establecer exactamente que, según afirmaba, su regeneración era un hecho real.

Con los elementos en nuestro poder se practicó una averiguación minuciosa, que nos dió la probanza de que esa mujer se halla alejada, desde hace más de cuatro años, de todo lo que, remotamente, podría tener relación con su triste pasado.-

Tuvimos la satisfacción de informar al

10. (continued)

Translation: Letter from the IWO (Jewish Scientific Institute) to the Polish Consulate in Buenos Aires in answer to a request for information regarding "the moral conduct and the means of subsistence of a certain Raquel Liberman":

"The name of Raquel Liberman is very well known for her participation in the case against the *Zwi Migdal*. Therefore it is not necessary to enter other considerations than those that pertain to us for the case we are about to present."

"The Polish Consulate has turned to our institution in order to request information regarding the moral conduct and the means of survival of a certain Raquel Liberman, who was requesting a travel visa. We have already pointed out on various opportunities that the Polish Consulate frequently seeks the services of our office to prove if those who have to travel to Poland are not part of that disreputable element."

"Once the steps were taken to identify the named woman, it was verified that they were referring to "La Liberman", whom we knew from the Migdal process. We were acquainted with her past history in all its details, but we wanted to find out about her present occupation. With the passage of time we lost sight of her, and were unaware of her activities."

"To carry out the research in a discreet manner would have presented the inconvenience of having to spend much more time than we had at our disposal. That prompted us to visit "La Liberman" at her home. No sooner had we crossed the threshold of her door that we received a pleasant impression. Anyone who saw her now, in this new, healthy surrounding, would be far from surmising that this was the same woman who had once spent a licentious life for several years. Nevertheless, the stigma generally leaves an indelible seal in the faces of many women who had the misfortune of surrendering themselves continuously to vicious practices."

"'La Liberman' made a favorable impression on us because it surely provides a very pleasant contrast with other redeemed women who in their new condition rekindled our interest to observe closely."

"Once we attended to the question of interest to us, "La Liberman" was very well disposed to provide all the information requested with the purpose of establishing exactly that, as she insisted, her regeneration was a real fact."

"With this information in our power, our careful investigation confirmed to us that that woman was away for more than four years, from all that could remotely have any relation with her sad past. It was our pleasure to provide the Polish Consulate with the results of our investigation."

REGISTRO CIVIL

REGISTRO CIVIL

GRATIS   Nº 005976

Buenos Aires, *Junio 1.* de 1935

Alberto Steffens Soler Jefe de *la Sección*
Cuarta del Registro Civil, certifica: que
en el tomo *primero* de los libros de
defunciones. existe un acta
que dice así:

"Número *Ciento cuarenta y nueve:*
En la Capital de la República Argenti-
na á nueve de Abril de mil novecien-
tos treinta y cinco, Ante mi Jefe de
la Sección Cuarta del Registro: E-
ladio Fernandez de treinta años, sol-
tero domiciliado Lamadrid cuatro-
cientos cincuenta y tres; declaró que
el siete del corriente á las trece en el
Hospital Argerich falleció Ruchla
Loja Liberman de bocio exoftámi-
co según certificado del médico Agus-
tín A Craviotto que archivó bajo el núme-
ro de esta acta, que era del sexo femenino,
y de treinta y siete años, polaca, domici-
liada Gallo ochocientos sesenta y
uno, hija de León Liberman ruso,
fallecido y de Elena Vaynerston

11. Death certificate for Raquel Liberman, Argerich Hospital,
Buenos Aires.

Leon Ferber. Se ignora si testó. Leída el acta la firmaron conmigo el declarante y el testigo Augusto Rodolfo Olivieri de treinta años, soltero, domiciliado en casa del declarante quienes han visto el cadaver. Eladio Fernandez. Augusto R. Olivieri. A. Steffen Soler. Hay un sello. A pedido de parte interesada expido el presente que sello y firmo en Buenos Aires, fecha ut retro "Enmendado ex of tamico vale"

11. *(continued)*

Translation: Death Certificate for Raquel Liberman at Argerich Hospital, Buenos Aires

Argentine Republic   No 005976

Buenos Aires, June 1, 1935

Alberto Steffen Soler, Chief ot the fourth section of the Civil Registry, certifies that in the first volume of the register of deaths there is a document that states the following:

Number 149. Issued at the Capital of the Argentine Republic on the 9th of April of 1935, before my Chief of the Fourth Section of the Register, Eladio Fernandez, thirty years old, single, living on Lamadrid Street number 453; he declared that on the 7th of this month at 1 p.m. at the Argerich Hospital, *Ruchla Laja Liberman* died of a exophtalmic goiter, according to the medical certificate issued by Dr. Agustin A. Craviotto, who archived it under the number of this document, stating that she was of the female sex, aged 37, Polish, living at Galli 861, daughter of León Liberman, Russian, decesased, and of Elena Vaynerton, Russian, living in Russia, and widow of Leon Ferber. It is not known if she left a will. After this statement was read, it was signed before me by the declarant and the witness Augusto Rodolfo Oliviero aged 35, single, living at the declarant's house, who saw the corpse.

Eladio Fernández. Augusto A. Oliveri, A. Steffen Soler.

There is a seal. At the request of the interested party I issue the following, which I seal and sign in Buenos Aires. (date . . .)

amendment of spelling of "exophtalmic" to "exoftamic". (sic)

DOCUMENTATION ON YAACOV FERBER:

1. Yaacov Ferber's passport issued in Poland, 3-5-1921
2. Health certificate for Yaacov Ferber, issued at the Argentine Consulate in Warsaw, July 4, 1921.
3. Work (Industrial aptitude) certificate for Yaacov Ferber as a tailor, Argentine Consulate in Warsaw July 4, 1921.
4. Certificate of good behavior issued to Yaacov Ferber, at the Argentine Consulate in Warsaw, July 4, 1921.
5. Certificate issued to Yaacov Ferber stating he is not indigent nor insane, July 4, 1921.
6. Passport issued to Yaacov Ferber by the Argentine Consulate in Warsaw, July 4, 1921. (2pp.)

1. Yaacov Ferber's passport issued in Poland, 3-5-1921.

2. Health certificate for Yaacov Ferber, issued at the Argentine
Consulate in Warsaw, July 4, 1921.

3. Work (Industrial aptitude) certificate for Yaacov Ferber as a tailor, Argentine Consulate in Warsaw July 4, 1921.

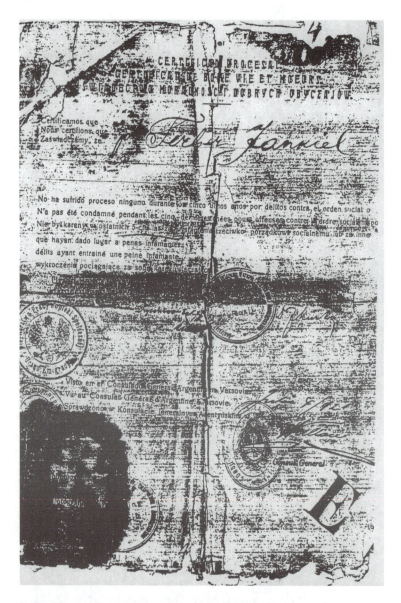

4. Certificate of good behavior issued to Yaacov Ferber, at the Argentine Consulate in Warsaw, July 4, 1921.

5. Certificate issued to Yaacov Ferber stating he is not indigent nor insane, July 4, 1921.

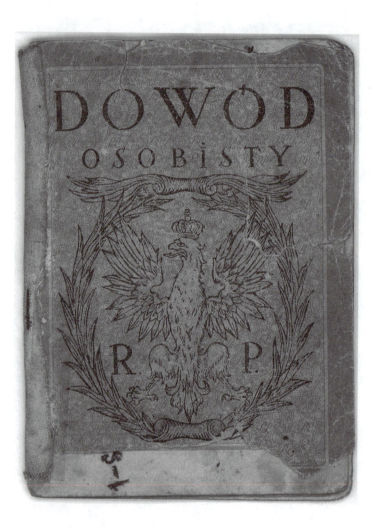

6. Passport issued to Yaacov Ferber by the Argentine Consulate in Warsaw, July 4, 1921. (2pp.)

6. *(continued)*

CHAPTER V

Correspondence

In the course of time the epistolary genre is moving towards oblivion. Facing twentieth century electronic bombardment in which the telephone, the fax, and E-mail, replace conventional mail so effectively, we should be happy that the paper of Raquel's letters has not disintegrated or even lost its color, as is the case with fax paper, and that her photos have not lost their lustre, as is the case with so many massively produced photo negatives.

There are various reasons why Raquel's letters* remained abandoned for over half a century. They were written in Yiddish, a language Raquel's children did not know. Yiddish represented a stigma they would rather deny: their anguishing relationship with the diaspora and with their European *shtetl*. Besides having grown up in a provincial village where there was not even a Jewish school, Raquel' children never had the chance to learn the Yiddish language. Her only surviving son—who never wanted to talk about his mother—preferred to keep the letters in a crate till after his death. His nephews, (Raquel's grandchildren), had the letters translated into Spanish.

What happened during the year of separation of the Liberman-Ferber couple, comes to life through their continuous correspondence written in a polished, literary Yiddish. The optimistic tone of some of the letters stems from the prospects for a happy life in a country that offers multiple opportunities for advancement. The letters reveal the love and the trust that exists between husband and wife.

At the same time, they are a proof of the great sadness that is caused by their being separated for so many months—from being unable to share the happiness of a family celebration and from missing the presence of the other partner during an illness. Both parties express great curiosity about the uncertainty of their future in a strange land: "How is life over there, in Argentina?" "What jobs are available?" They ask themselves questions, that are in their majority centered upon their intimate life. They care little about their external world. Yaacov expresses curiosity to find out who was the *sandek* (the man who held the baby in his arms) during the ceremony. He is anxious to find out if his older son got over his illness completely; he asks how his relatives are treating his wife, what is her money situation.

As time passes the insistence of Raquel to receive the money for the tickets increases. The complaints, gentle at the beginning, become graver; the recriminations, more eloquent. Raquel implores her husband to intercede in her favor so that her sister-in-law Helke takes pity on her terrible situation, liberates her from the prison where she is confined (referring to her own sister's house in Warsaw) and finances her tickets to Buenos Aires. Finally she appeals to her own sister-in-law to rescue her.

Although Raquel is pleased to hear that her husband is adapting to his new milieu and that he plans a home for them, she nevertheless, fears to be displaced by her sister-in-law. One could speculate that Raquel feared that Yaacov would not hurry enough to send for her, as was the case with many husbands who, having settled in America, abandoned their spouses in Europe. Nevertheless, in this case, the correspondence of the couple seems to indicate the opposite. Of the two, the one who appears the stronger, is Raquel with her categorical and insistent character.

During the very short time in which Yaacov held a job in Cacharí, his happiness was boundless. He expresses it in a romantic and graphic metaphor:

> Until now our luck was bleak and water reached almost to the neck. As they say, "until there is light, darkness must be total. Then, suddenly, a little light appears that gets bigger and bigger." With God's help, I pray that soon will come the end of all of our sorrows and of the anguish we have been suffering.

Nevertheless, Yaacov's financial success was ephemeral. The illness he suffered, almost from his arrival in Argentina, frustrated all his plans.

Justifiably, health is one of the couple's preoccupations. At the beginning, Raquel writes of her son's illness, which was a cause of anguish for Yaacov, and he, in turn, tells his wife of his ailments. Although Yaacov writes at every opportunity that he is undergoing medical treatment in Buenos Aires—first helped by a witch-doctor, and then by a certified physician—Raquel cannot determine how serious her husband's illness is. For her part, she assures him in a letter that her son has recovered. She admits that the fact that her family in Lodz is enjoying good health is a miracle in itself, but she adds skeptically, that "not every day a miracle takes place . . . [and that] The strength weakens from so much pain . . . Can the milk that nurses my son keep flowing from a desperate heart?" Perhaps Raquel foresaw intuitively the danger that threatened her husband and strove to get to Buenos Aires and find him still alive. And from there stems her insistence to receive the fare for her tickets.

Another conjecture is that Raquel may have wanted to assure herself at all cost that she could emigrate with her children without any obstacles. Many families that separated at similar occasions were never reunited.

One of the worst fears that assailed Yaacov was that his wife could find herself in need to ask for Jewish charity. The couple's exchange of letters ends precisely when Yaacov sends Raquel the money that is provided by his sister Helke. Curiously, what stands out at this occasion is Yaacov's integrity, when he insists that his wife does not leave Poland without having paid all the pending debts. *Has vechalila* (spare the thought!) I wouldn't want you to leave while still owing money to anybody!"

In one of her letters: Raquel complains that Yaacov's arrival in Argentina has not helped to improve her situation, since on either side of the ocean, she still depends on the charity of her relatives.

OTHER LETTERS:

After her arrival, Raquel and her sister-in-law take turns to look after Yaacov in hospital. Their visits are spaced in time due to the high cost of travel to the capital. The last reference to Yaacov's hospitalization in Buenos Aires is a letter from Helke dated July 27, 1923. In this letter Helke describes to Yaacov the mixture of fear and of relief that provoked the screams of his relatives in Talpalqué: *Got, helf!* (God, help!). This time it is Helke who sends greetings to Yaacov on behalf of his wife Raquel, his children, his friends and neighbors, all of whom pray for his health. Yaacov Ferber dies in the same year, 1923.

The last letter addressed to Raquel was written on Nov. 3, 1933. It was sent by a friend—Eugenia Elisa—who was living in Raquel's apartment, taking care of her children. This brief letter is important because it refers to Raquel's constant preoccupation with the health and education of her children. Her friend tries to comfort Raquel by assuring her that the children behave well and that they study. She also asks her not to be offended if she does not answer her letters immediately. At this time, after the failure of Raquel's business at Callao Street she is determined to try again. In this letter, her friend lets Raquel know that on the first of the month the new shop will be available, and advises her to wait patiently ("all will be sorted out.")

Two brief notes arrived from Raquel's children on the same date. They express the great love they feel for their mother and their desire to see her as soon as possible.

The series of letters between Raquel and Yaacov rescues a lost genre and reveals Raquel's most noble aspect: her eloquent voice, her vibrant, clear style, her correct Yiddish grammar, her careful calligraphy. The education Raquel received at "Jerusalem", her Yiddish school in Warsaw, was of a high level. Her mastery of the Yiddish language and of Jewish history are always evident by the ease with which she incorporates them into her Yiddish. Her familiarity with the Hebrew calendar and with Jewish festivities can be seen in her various letters. The information given in the letters is of great value, since it permits the reader to appreciate the deep concern that Raquel felt for her children. Any conjecture regarding the reasons that drove her to prostitution is related to her circumstances.

*The original letters follow each translated letter.

I. LETTERS TRANSLATED FROM YIDDISH INTO ENGLISH:

L. Raquel to Yaacov:

(Praise the Lord) Warsaw, Tuesday . . .

My dear husband:

I'm writing to you about our health and of our dear son's health, so you know, my dear husband, that I don't want to wait until I receive your letter from Argentina. I write to you in the meanwhile, since my time here, without you becomes too long, I busy myself this way, as this is a consolation for me. I tell you, my dear husband, that I have taken a photograph of our dear son, and I'll send it to you soon. I'd also like to tell you that our little one shouts "Papa" at our brother-in-law, because he hears his cousins calling him "Papa".

My dear husband, I beg you to keep sending me your letters and good news. Write to me about the trip, how it went. When you get off the boat, tell me how you felt on board. If you felt sick, everything . . . You can imagine the mood I'm in. I receive 3000 marks a week from my brother-in-law Shaie. He told me he'd give me more if he could afford it, but he can't just now. If he gave me anymore it would be good for me and for my son, because prices go up everyday and money goes on sugar, milk and food. I eat with my in-laws.

Dear husband; I don't have to tell it to you nor to repeat it to you, since you are a faithful husband and I am a faithful wife *to hurry your papers* and see what you can do so we can reunite soon. Our dear son sends you kisses from here. The same with your in-laws, who are eager to see that my children and myself don't have to be separated from you for much longer.

Kisses, adieu, Raquel

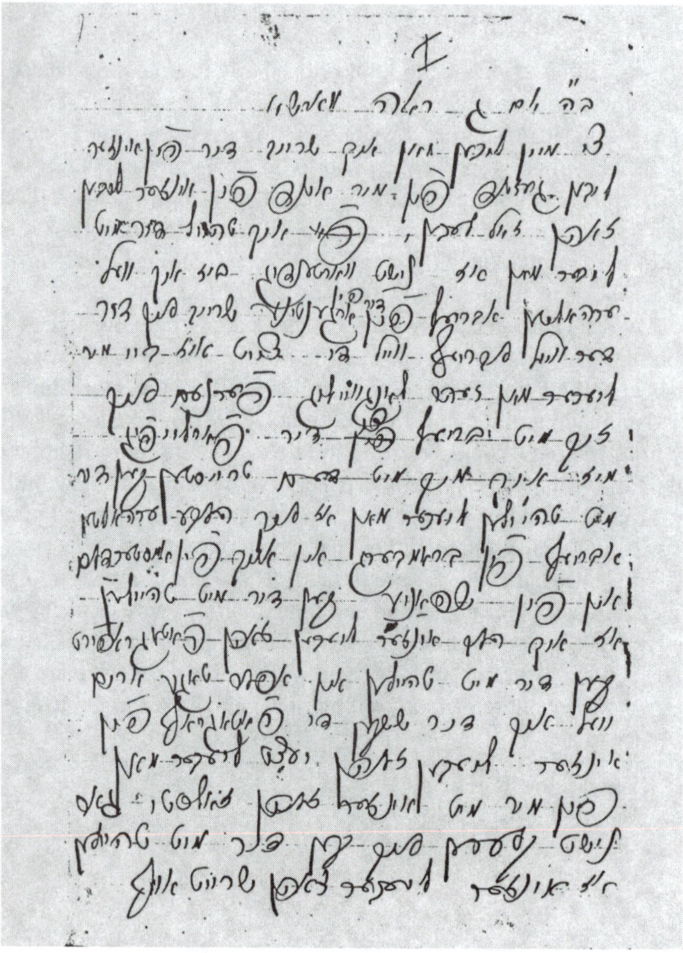

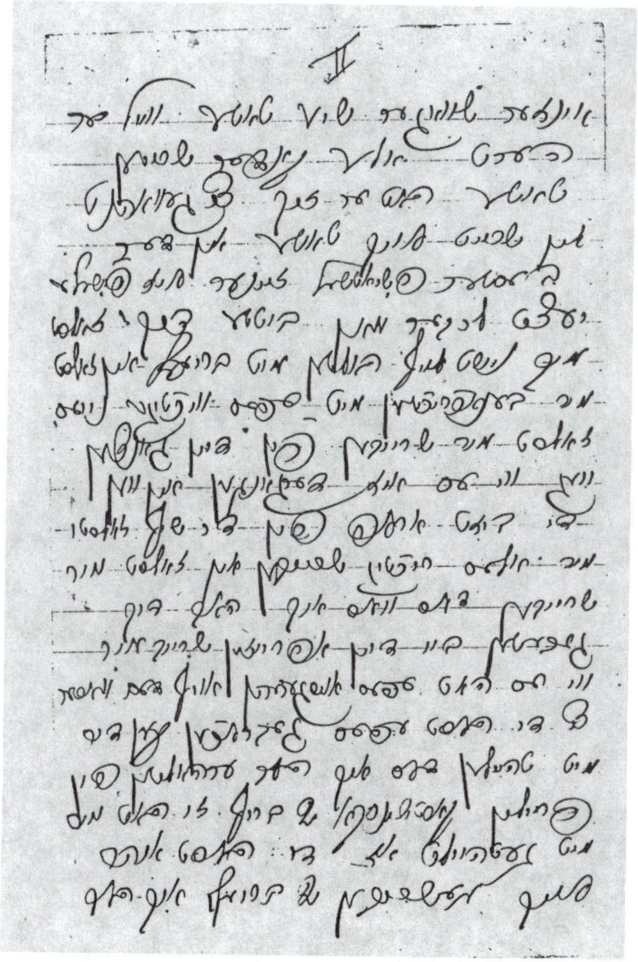

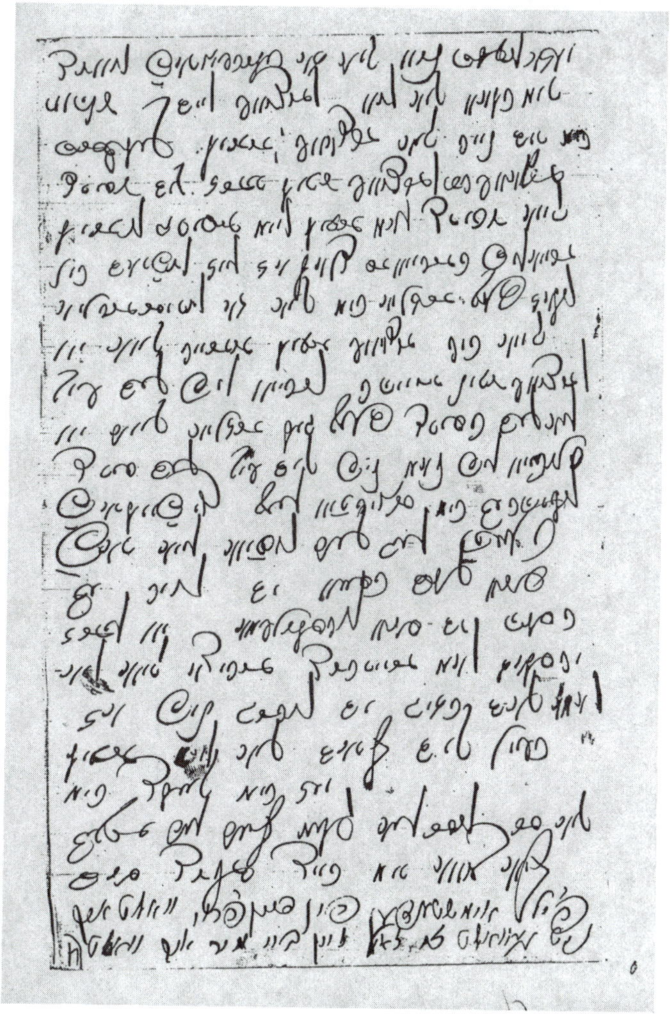

2. Yaacov's Photo and Letter and from the Ship

On board,

I'm sending you the second postcard from the boat, where we took photographs in Marseilles. How are you and how is our son? Send me photographs.

Your husband, who hopes to see you son . . . as soon as possible,

Yaacov Ferber

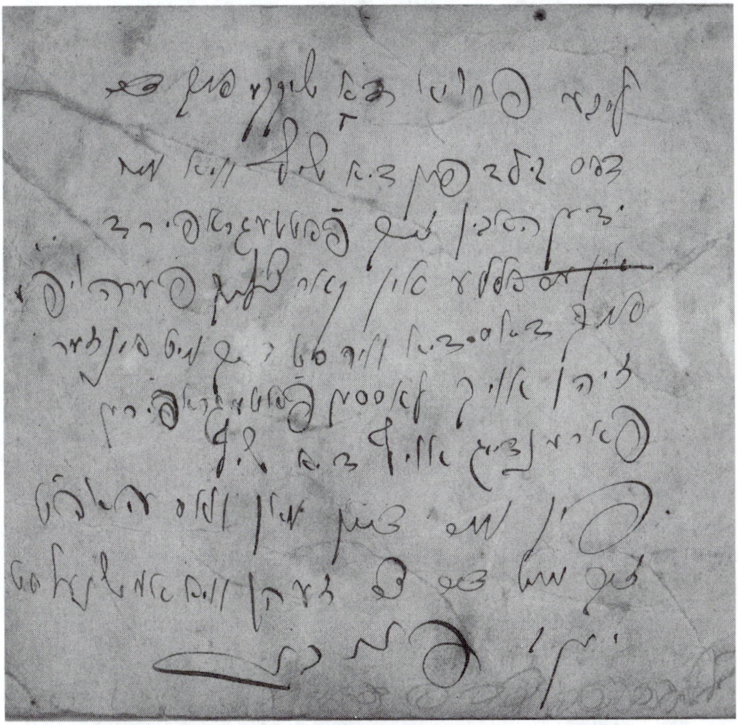

Yaacov Ferber in Marseille, France, on route to Argentina, 1921.

3. Yaacov Sends a Postcard to Raquel from the Ship:

Tisha b' Ab, Sunday morning, August 15, 1921

My dear wife and dear son:

We arrived in Spain. The boat is anchored. More passengers are coming up. At 12 we leave for Portugal. May God help me and may I be in good health throughout the trip, not so much for myself as for my son. Hugs and kisses from you faithful husband, hopeful to meet you soon. Kisses to you and our dear son from far away,

Dear in-laws. I greet you with great affection. Dear wife and dear son, I'm keeping well, thank God.

Adieu, adieu, Yaacov

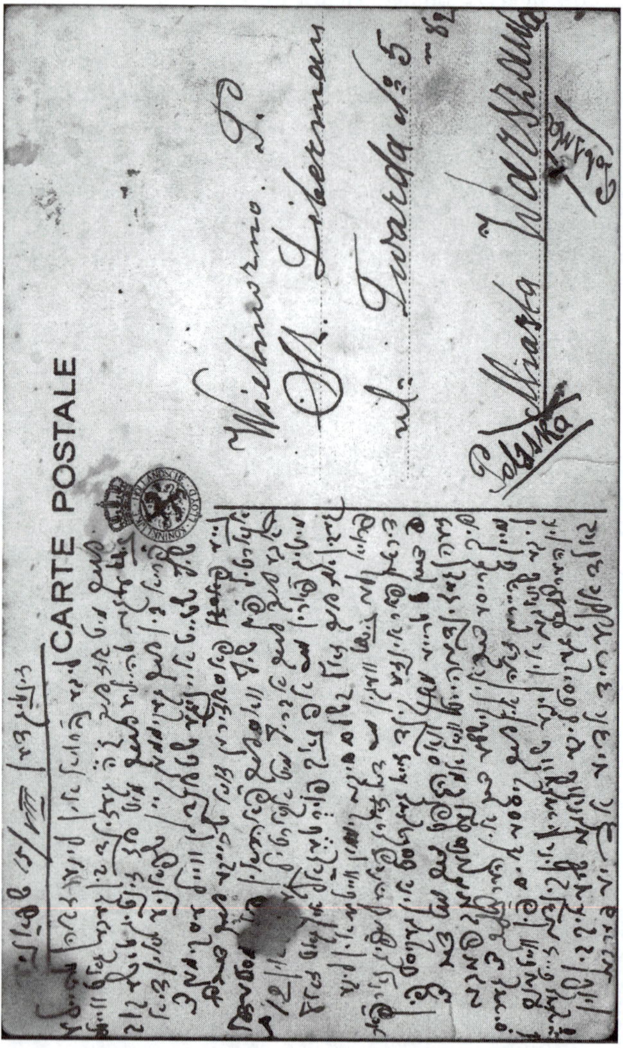
CARTE POSTALE

4. Yaacov to Raquel : (Part of this letter is missing)

Tapalqué . . .

Ask his family and charge it to his account. She will most probably visit you, and ask her to go with her to the Courthouse. I hope you go with her, so you'll also have a chance to amuse yourself with the thought that I almost got killed. A month before I came to Buenos Aires, her husband's sister sent 20,000 German marks to cover your expenses. Don't forget to send me Raise's London address. Please send me more photographs, and if our son does not want to pose by himself, please stay next to him.

I don't have a steady job, but I do whatever comes my way. I have tailored a black suit for my brother-in-law, and for myself a dark red suit for the festivities. I have also purchased a pair of patent leather shoes and a foreign-made hat, because I looked too much like a *gringo* in my *kapelush* hat. They put aside the clothes I was wearing as soon as I arrived. Before my arrival they had already prepared for me clothes made of silk. Silk on the inside and silk in the lining. It would cost a fortune in Poland. I lack nothing. I only wish you and my dear son were here with me.

Not far from here there is a lake where I go fishing the entire day. And if I don't fish, there are horse-carriages, which I tie, and spend a few hours there. My main task here now is to learn the language. The only cause for my suffering is to know you are not well. But with God's help you'll be at my side and then we'll be able to live the life we deserve.

I end my letter with a great hug from your husband that hopes to see you and our son, and some more. I greet you and our beloved son and I kiss you both from afar. I also greet my dear brother-in-law Shaie and my sister-in-law Chavele and her children. A warm greeting to my sister-in-law Rivkele and her husband and children. A warm greeting to my cousin Chavele and her husband Yidl. A warm greeting to my sister Daniela. Let her write to me how she is doing. I also send a greeting to Yindele and her husband, and to my cousin Guitele and her fiancé. Ask Yindele and Guitele and fiancé to send me their photos, and if they do I will be very grateful and send them photos from here. I'm also sending you a peso so that you can see what Argentine money looks like. But don't throw it away because here they pay 1.200 Polish marks for every peso. Write to me about everything. What they are talking about in Warsaw. Has the cold weather started there? Here, in Tapalqué, Spring has started already on October 1 and the trees are blooming, just the same as in our country after Passover.

Adieu, Yaacov Ferber

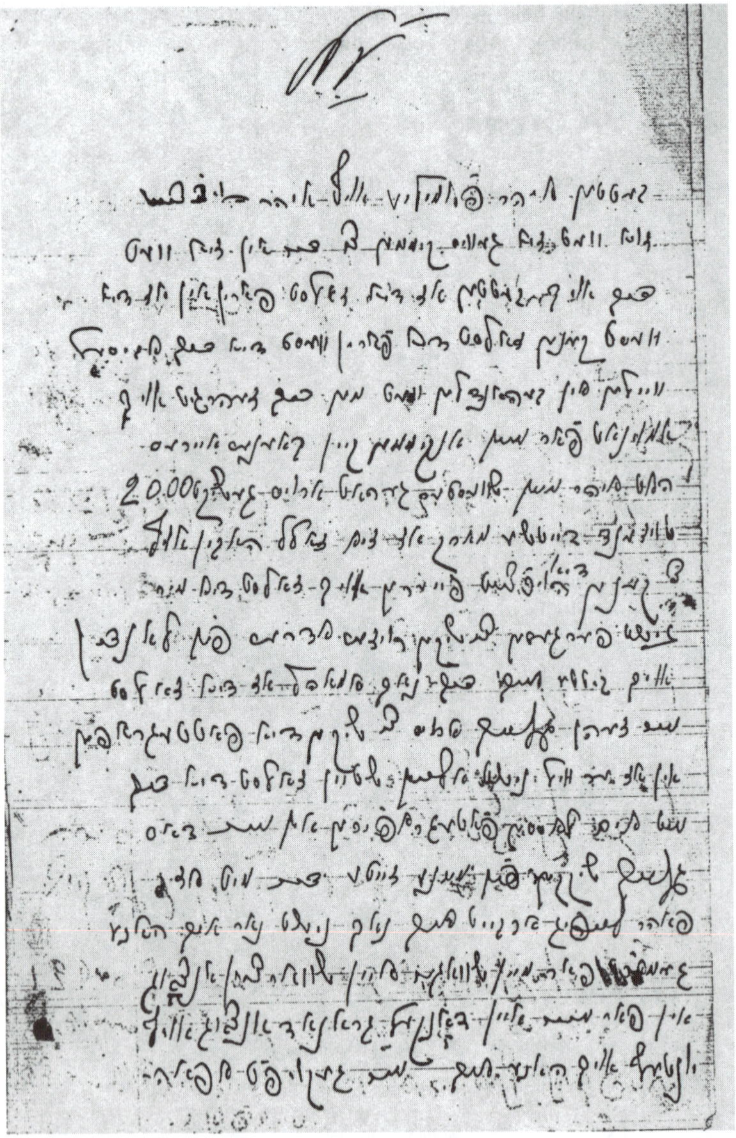

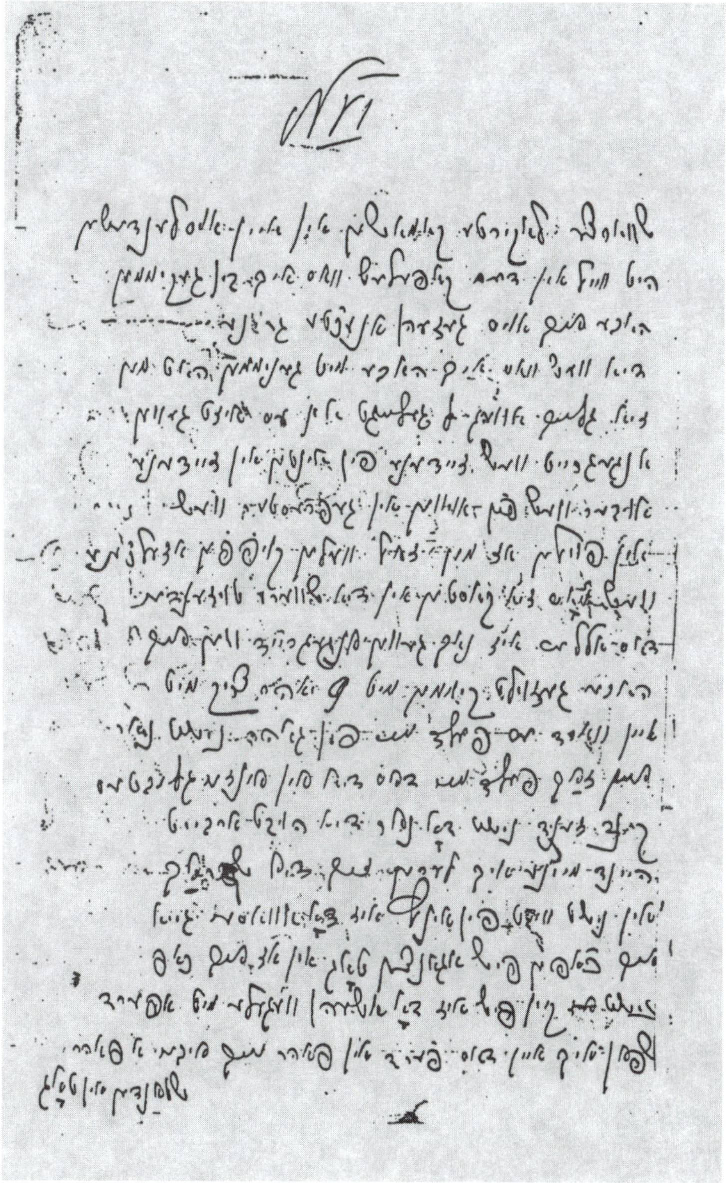

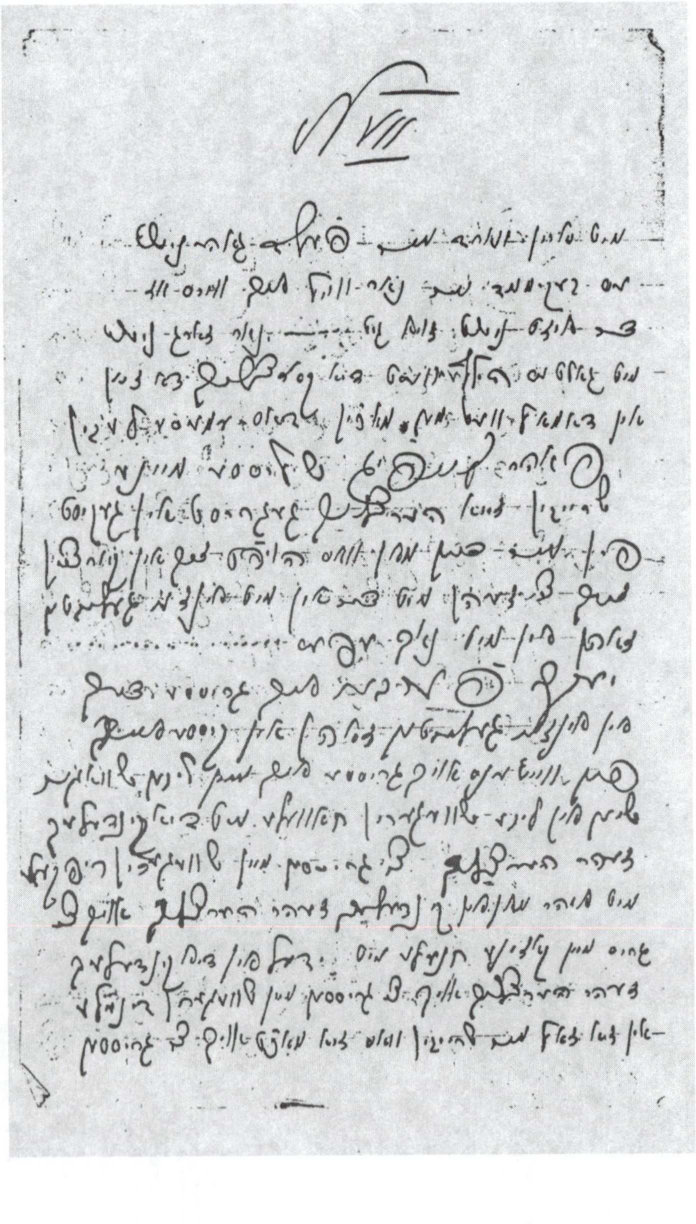

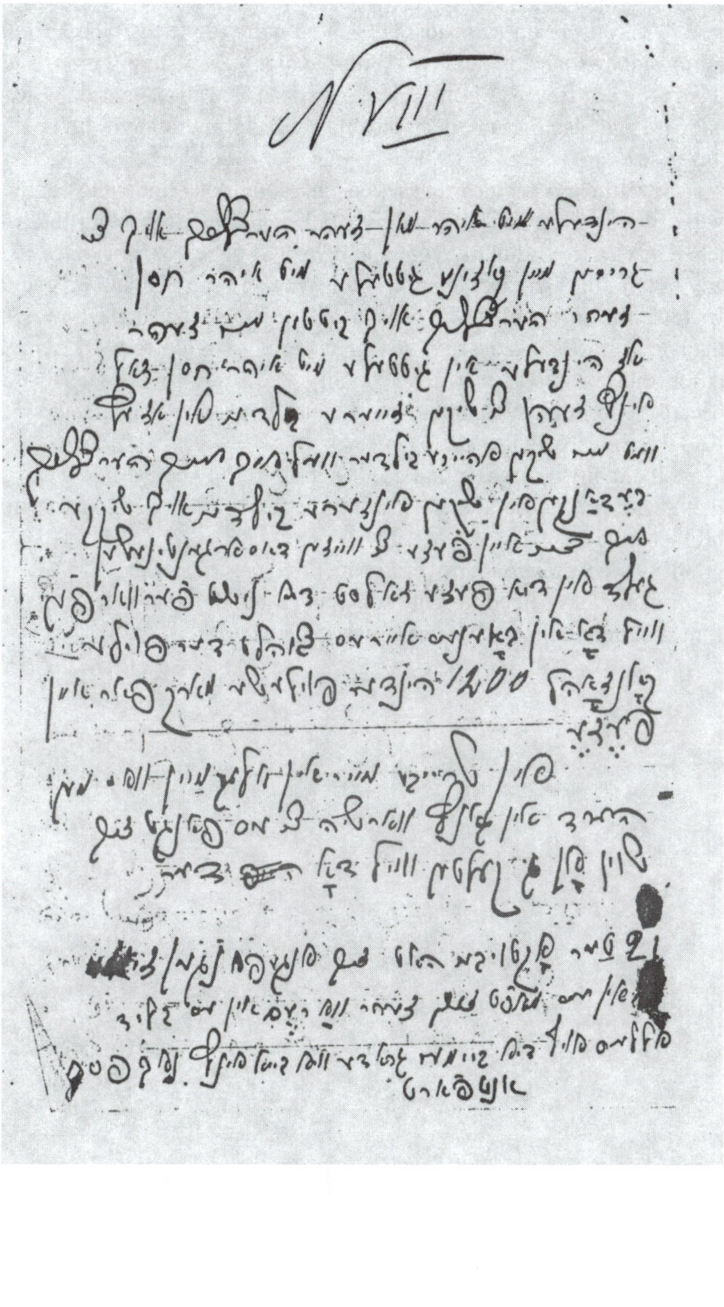

5. Yaacov to Raquel: (Four pages are missing)

. . . so you never know of losses . . . You write to me that you spent a lot of money for your sickness. With the high cost of living in Poland, this is a great tragedy. I only thank our dear God that the money was enough, and also that my dear cousins Yidl and my relatives helped in this case.

Nevertheless, my dear ones, you can see I do my utmost to comply with my duty as a husband and as a father. I know full well I did not leave there a lover, but my wife and my son. I believe I have acted like any faithful husband would act with his wife and son. Now I beg you to write to me in detail how you and all the others feel, and how you manage with the *parnoseh*. As for myself, I started to work with a tailor, but I worked for two weeks only, and I don't work any longer because I don't understand the language and they don't understand me. And the pay is very low.

I thank my dear sister and brother-in-law. They beg you to write to them with all the details. I close this letter with greetings from my brother-in-law.

I'm expecting your answer impatiently, Yaacov Ferber.

I would have liked to write some more, but the train is leaving and I must hasten to the post-office. Answer soon.

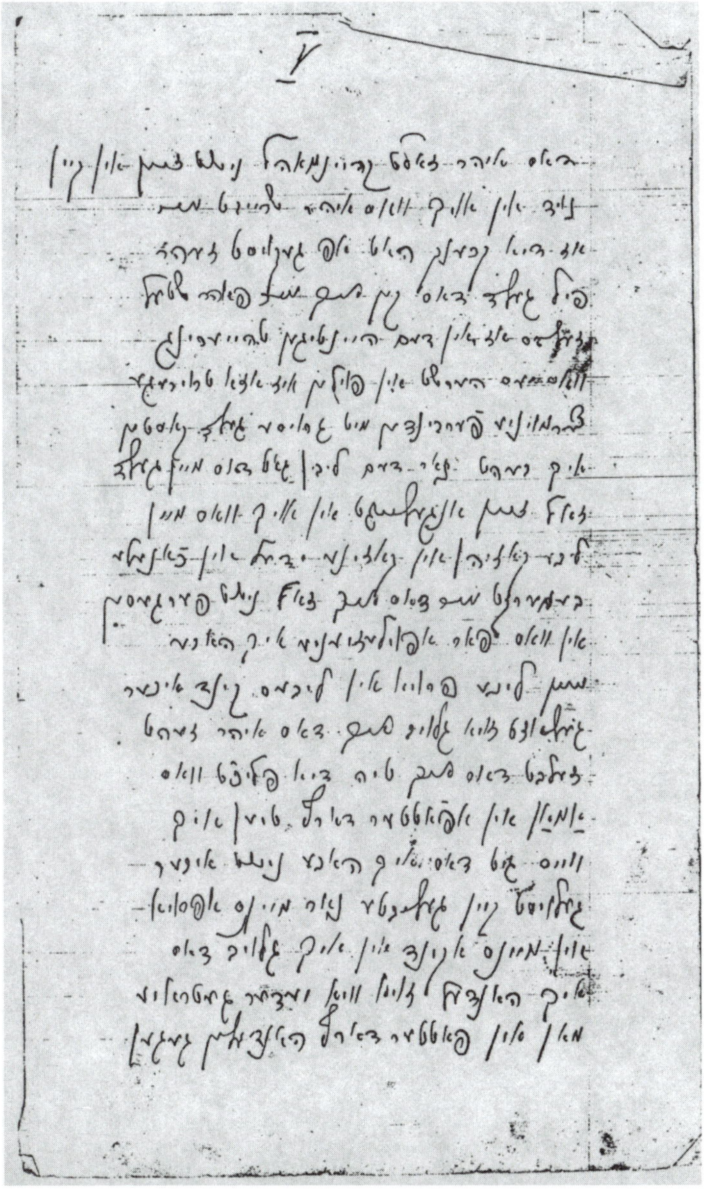

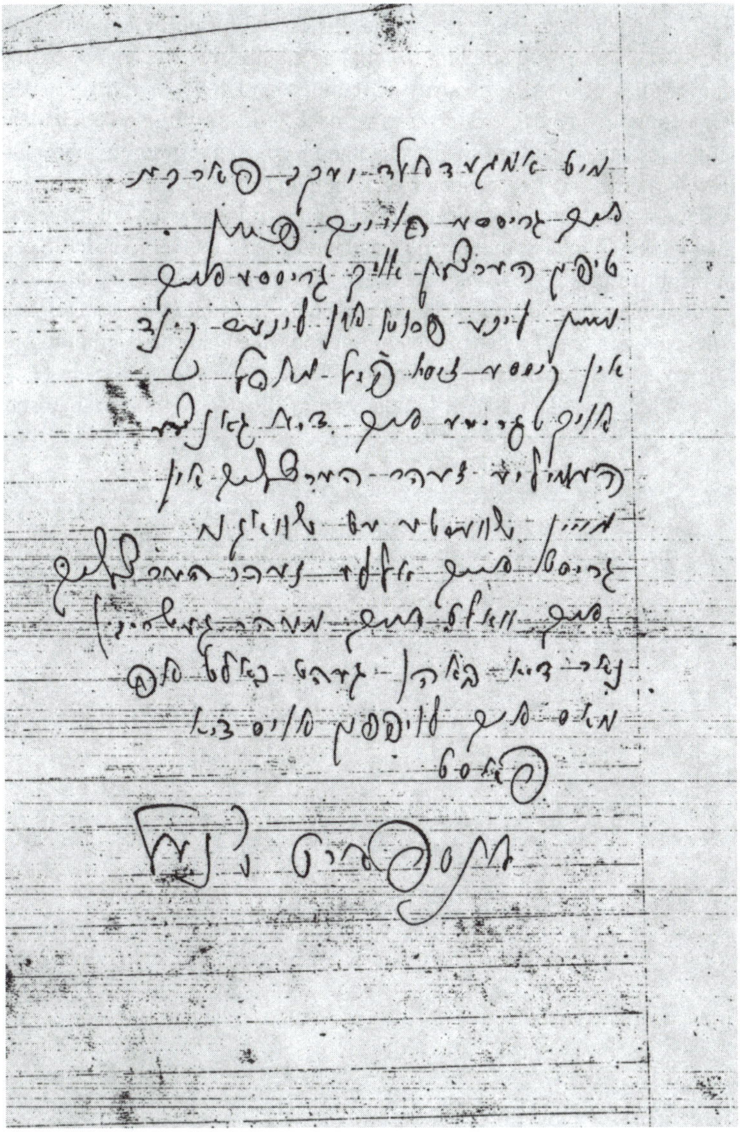

6. Yaacov to Raquel [Pages missing]

. . . A warm greeting to our son Shaie David. I kiss you a thousand times and I wish you and him a complete and fast recovery. Please send me Dudl's photos right away. Greetings and love to the relatives: Greetings to my dear sister-in-law and brother-in law and their dear children. May God give them health and *parnoseh*. I greet my sister-in-law Rifkele and her husband and their children. I greet my cousin Chavele and her husband Yidl. And I greet my sister-in-law Dineleh. My cousin Yindeleh and her husband, and I wish them a happy life and a bright future. I greet the Freindlich family. And now my dear sister and brother-in send you and your son Shaie Dudl many greetings. And she asks you to send her photos of our son. She also sends greetings to the cousins and the rest of the family. Please answer soon.

When my sister sent you money from Buenos Aires, she also sent you a letter. Tell me if you received it.

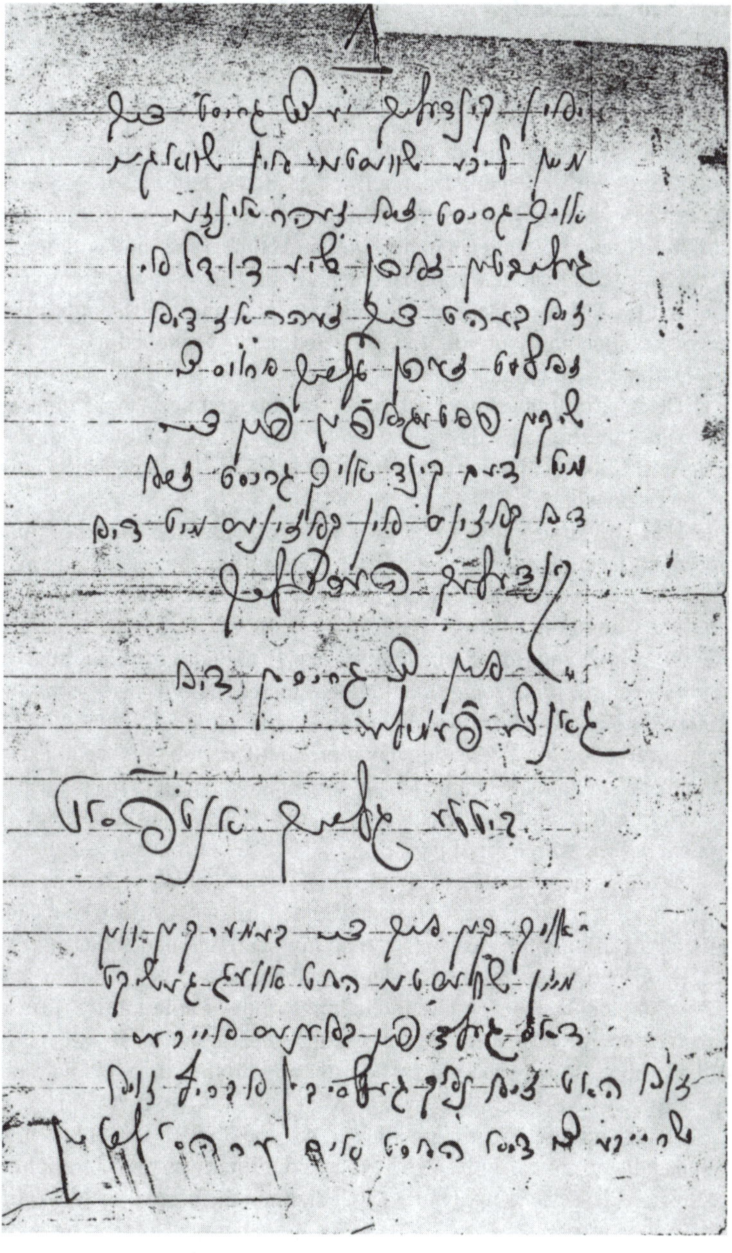

7. Yaacov to Raquel:

Tapalqué, December 8, 1921

Dear Wife, dear Children:

I want to let you know I'm feeling fine, and I hope and wish that my letter finds you all well. Dear wife: l read the letter in which you describe with every detail how things are going for you with our children. I read it with tears in my eyes, and at the same time with joy.

Dear wife: I can tell you that when my brother-in-law wrote to me the first time of the illness of our son, I suffered enormously; I felt my heart was bleeding; but your letter quieted me and relieved me. I hope God will keep on helping us.

Dear wife: Regarding what you write that you need more money, I'm sure that the same day you wrote to me—or the following day— you must have received my check for 33.- dollars. Please let me know if you received it.

I'd like you to know, my dear, that I sent you three checks so that you don't lack money. I wouldn't want, God forbid, that the community should have to keep you. You are my wife, and I have to worry that you don't lack anything.

I received your letter when my sister was about to travel to Buenos Aires, so she'll send you this letter from there, and will also send you 100 pesos - I don't know if in dollars or in British pounds.

Forgive me for not writing any more, but I want this letter to leave already. Write to me when you begin to prepare the papers for the trip.

Figure that within a few weeks you'll receive the third check. I hope it will be with a lot of luck.

Write to me what you're doing, and how our son is progressing.
I end my letter with warm hugs and kisses from your dear husband, who is awaiting your answer. Love to my dear son, and thousands of kisses. Greetings to my brother-in-law Shaie and to my sister-in-law Chaveleh, and to their children. Greetings to the whole family. Please forgive me for not writing to each one separately, as my sister is already about to take the train. My sister and brother-in-law send their greetings. Adieu, Yaacov.

[Pages missing] Warm greetings to our son Shaie David. I kiss him thousands of times and I wish you and him a fast and complete recovery! Please send my photos of Dudl. Send them right away. Warm greetings to my sister-in-law Shaie and my sister in law Chaveleh and their children. May our good God send them health and good business. Greetings to my sister-in-law Rifkele and her husband and children. Greetings to our sister Chaveleh and her husband Yidl and their children. Greetings to my sister Dineleh, my cousin Yindeleh, greetings to Masheleh, and her husband and children. And now my dear sister and brother-in-law greet you, and they send their love to our son Shaie Dudl, and they send photos of yourself and our dear son. Answer right back. Note: When my sister sent you the money from Buenos Aires, she also sent you a letter. Write to me if you received it.

Tapalque 8/12 1921

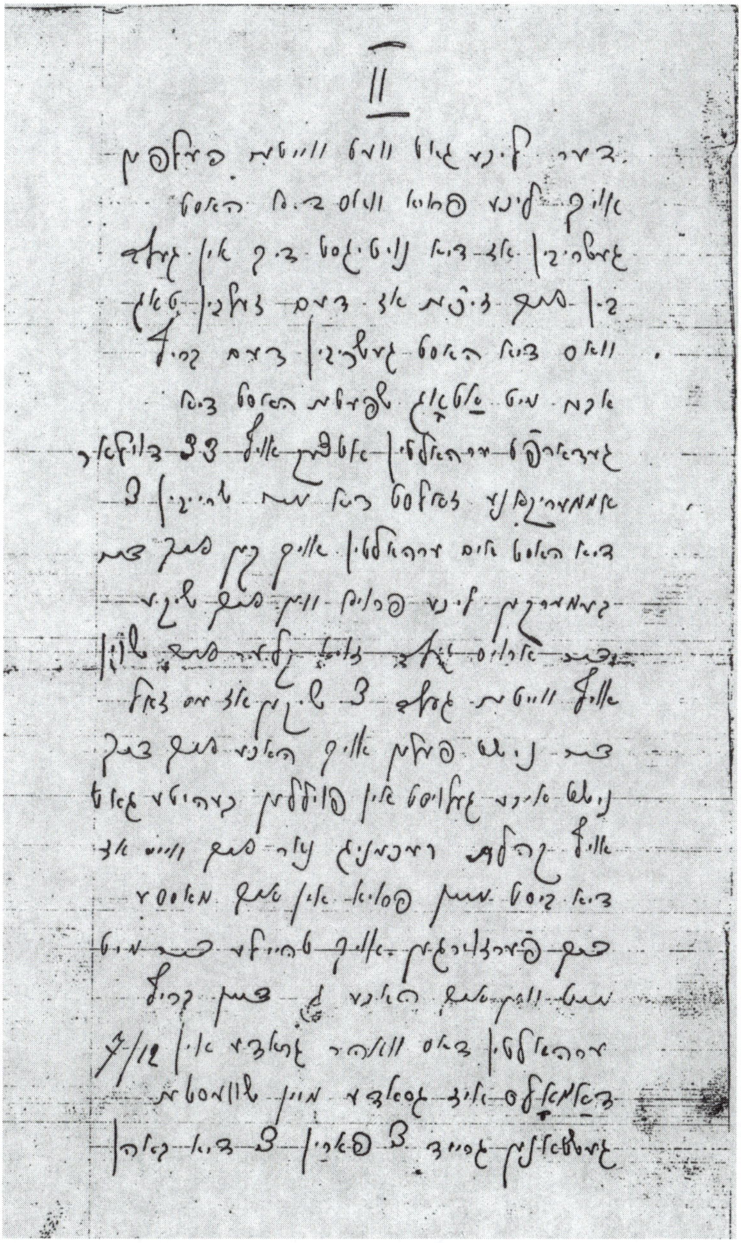

II

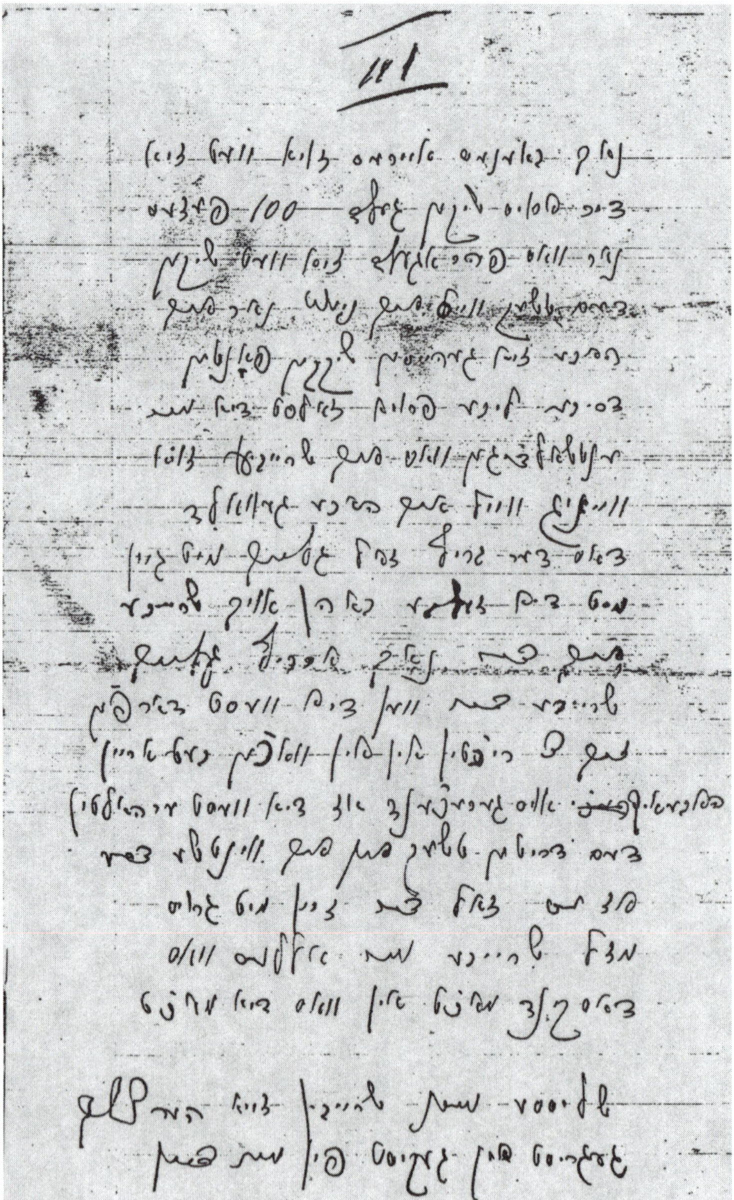

8. Yaacov to Raquel:

Cacharí, February 29, 1922.

My dear wife and dear children:
I received your letter and with great joy I read that, thank God, you are in good health. Now, my dear wife, you can congratulate me because on February 27, I entered, luckily, in *Gelepas* and may God help us, I am in good health. Because, my dear wife, until now our luck was very bleak, and the water came almost to the neck. But, how does the saying go? Until a little brightness appears, that grows and grows, it's darkest just before dawn. Suddenly a small light comes up, that becomes ever larger and with the help of God, I hope, all our sorrows and our anguish will end soon.

You know how much I despair being apart from you. Do you believe maybe, that my heart did not suffer enough when I found out from far away, about the illness of my son? Do you think maybe that when you gave birth—*in a gute shoo* (at a happy hour)to our son Moshe Velvele, and I could not participate in the celebration of his *brit mila* (circumcision), my heart did not bleed? But, dear wife, let us put aside our sorrows because the little light that is opening up for us gives me hope that all of the pain will end soon.

My faithful wife, until you have crossed the ocean, with good fortune, you will have to make a few more sacrifices. Do not let the journey scare you. You will come soon, with God's help.

I am hopeful that by the first of the fourth month I'll be able to travel to Buenos Aires and send you the passports, tickets and money, so you can pay all your debts there.

I also sent you a letter, my dear, and I wrote to you about my health all that time. At the beginning a healer told me my troubles were caused by the evil eye. And I think she was right on the mark because I already feel, thank God, almost well. I hope to be completely well soon.

Kisses from Yaacov.

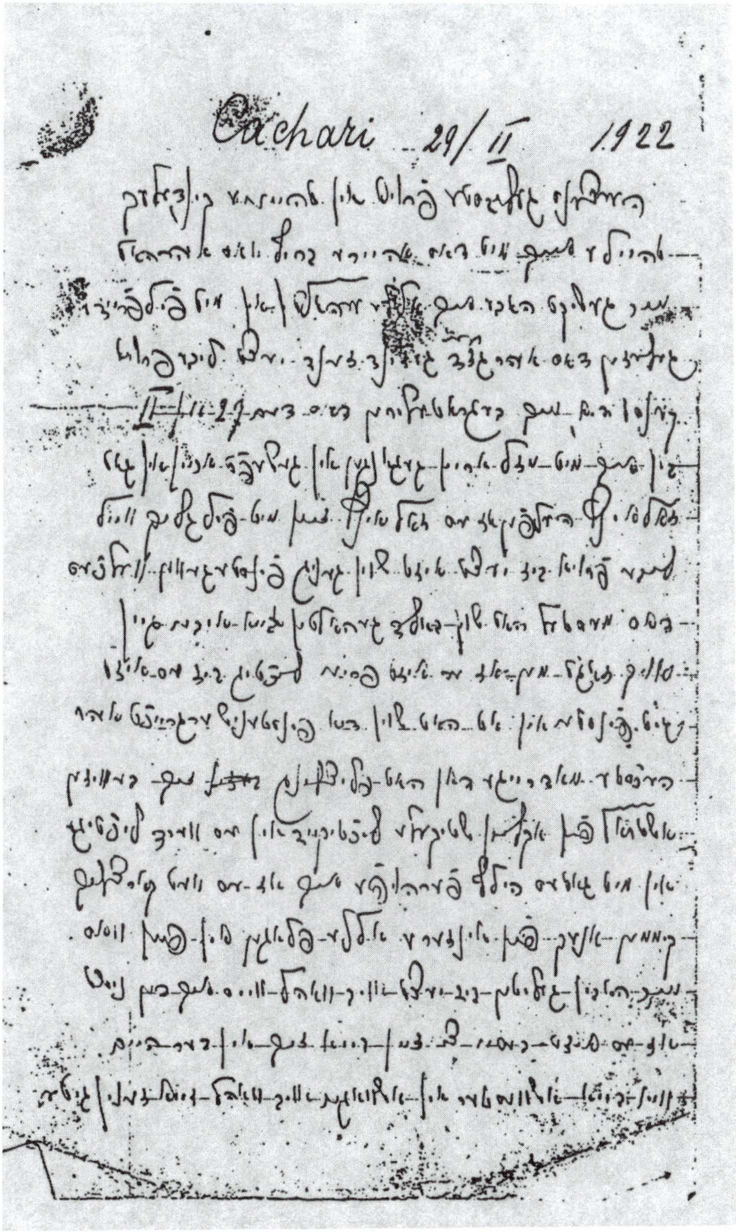
Cachari 29/II 1922

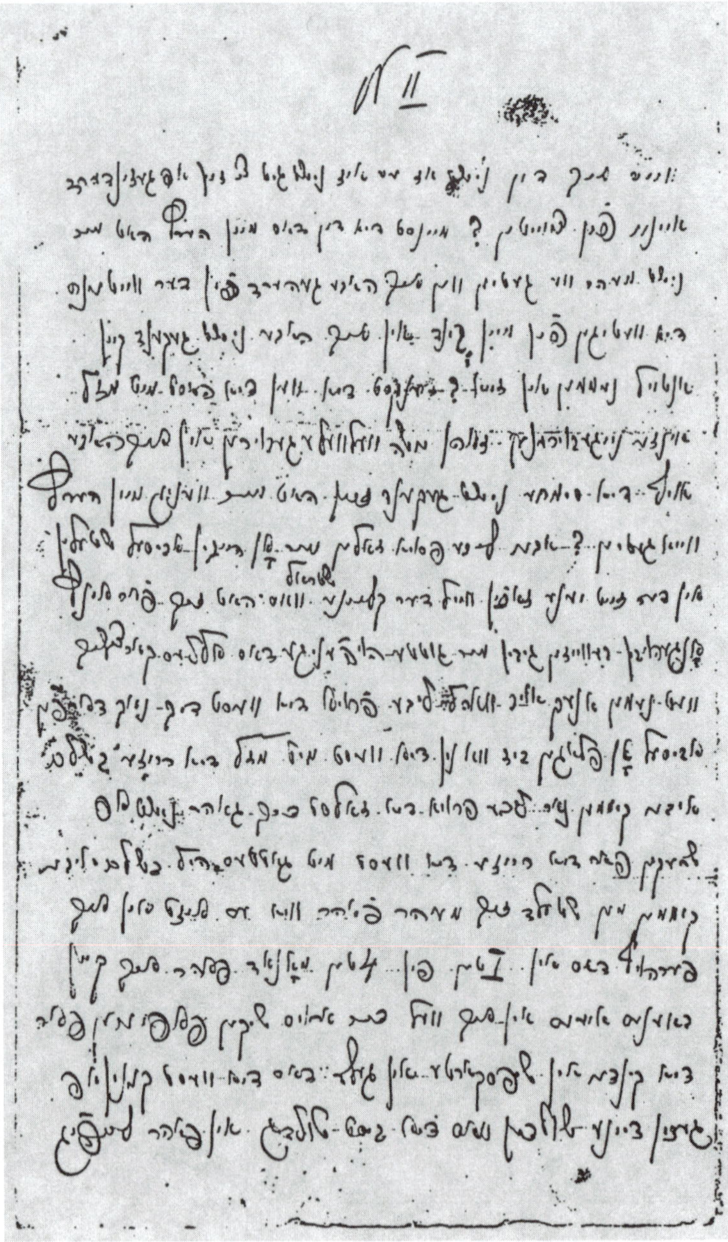

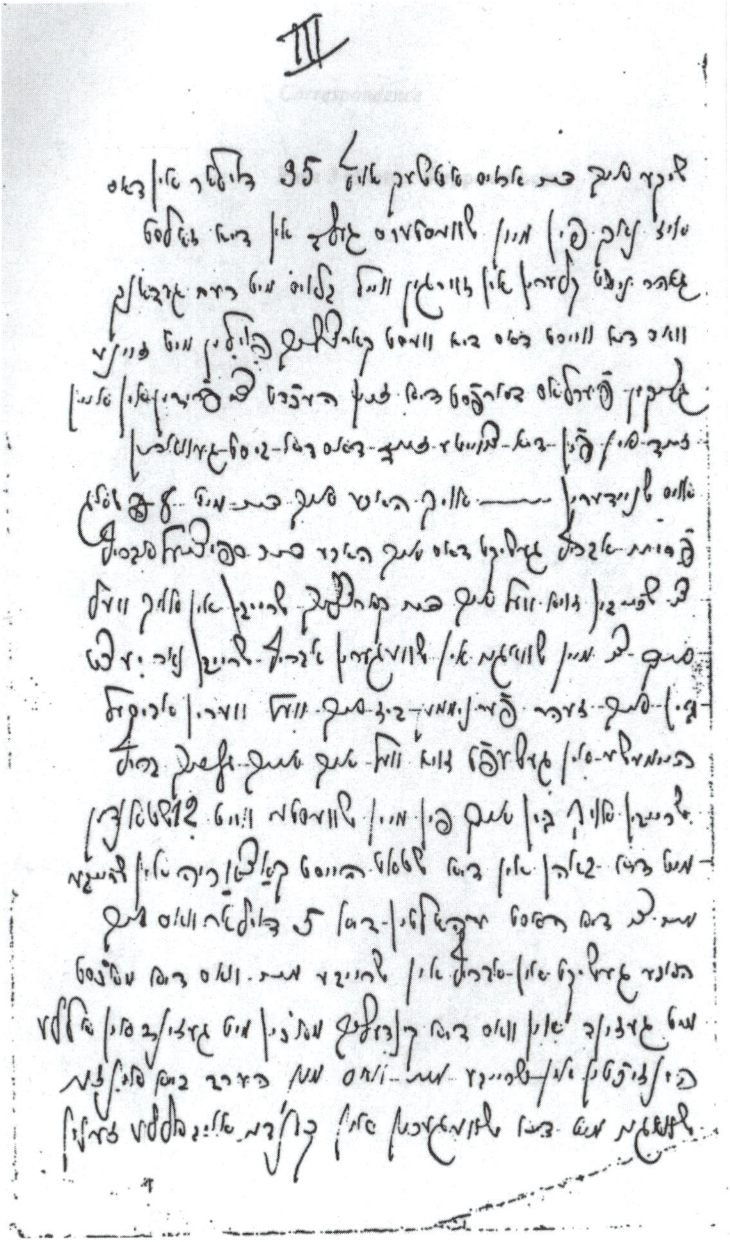

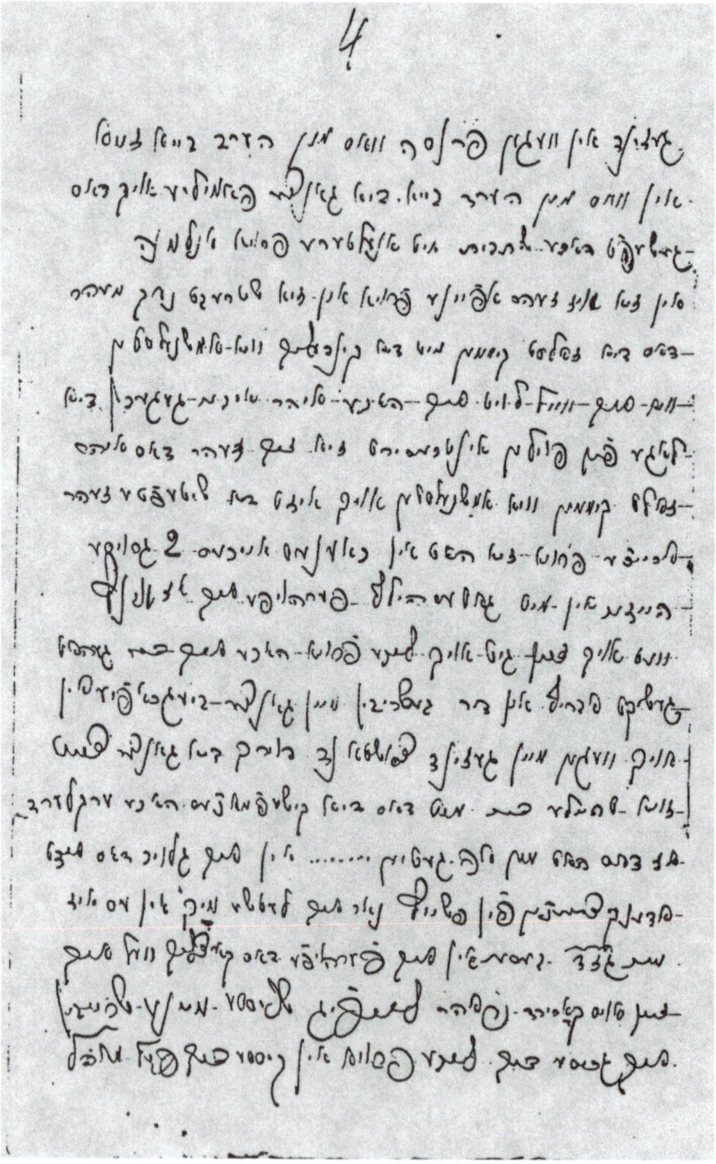

9. Yaacov to Raquel: Second Letter from Cacharí, Argentina.

Cacharí, March 1922

If the Argentine Council asks for the address of the person waiting for you, give her the following:
"Mr. Yaacov Ferber, Cacharí F.C.R.A. [Argentine Railroad]"
When you receive the cheque for 63.50 (Sixty three dollars and fifty cents), dear wife, you should distribute all of it as I told you, and keep me posted. You should take all you need for the trip, and you well know what that is because it's the same you gave me for my trip. Whatever else you need you can get on board. The name of the boat is *Kad Polonia*. I end my letter now. I'll write all the details as soon as I arrive home. A strong kiss to you and kisses to our dear children. Your husband who wants to be with you soon in good health, Yaacov Ferber.

Regards to your sister and brother-in-law, and their children, and regards to your sister Rivkele and to her husband and children, and regards to Dinele and husband and my cousin Javele and her husband and children, and regards to the whole family, my sister and brother-in-law; send them many regards. Also my sister received a letter . . .

Please answer right away; I'll write another letter to the port. It's better that you and the children come in a boat that covers the distance faster, You will be travelling through Hamburg. Try to travel in a boat named *Polonia* because this is one of the best ships in the world, and in the boat you can get a bedroom for yourself alone, because I've paid for it.

I can also recommend that when you hand in the luggage, you should take the tickets with you. And when you arrive to the port you should check well to see that the luggage arrived. Ask them to give you a pillow and a blanket, especially for the children, because at night it's cold in the boat. And when you're on board the ship ask them for milk for the children. And if you feel *halila* (God forbid) seasick, call the nurse in the hospital to take care of you and of the children, so they lack nothing. The crew is very good and they don't charge for their favors. And if they give you something you have to pay for, tell them that your husband will pay for everything when he comes to greet you at the port.

Also try not to remain without money in the trip. In case you wish to drink a glass of beer or another drink and buy chocolate and oranges for the boys, at least you should have ten dollars when you go on board for a long journey. And at each stop the boat makes, you'll see that children approach the boat in small rafts and you can buy everthing from them!

Don't be frightened if you get seasick. Try to have warm clothes for the children, and for yourself. Don't sell your clothes; pack everything, clothes and household items. Buy yourself and the children coats and shoes. And when you come out of this trip *beshalom* (in peace) I'll buy you such clothes that noone will guess you're a *greene* (foreigner) but that you are a native.

Señor. Jacobo. Ferber

    Cachari F.C. ... R. Argentina

Rad Palania

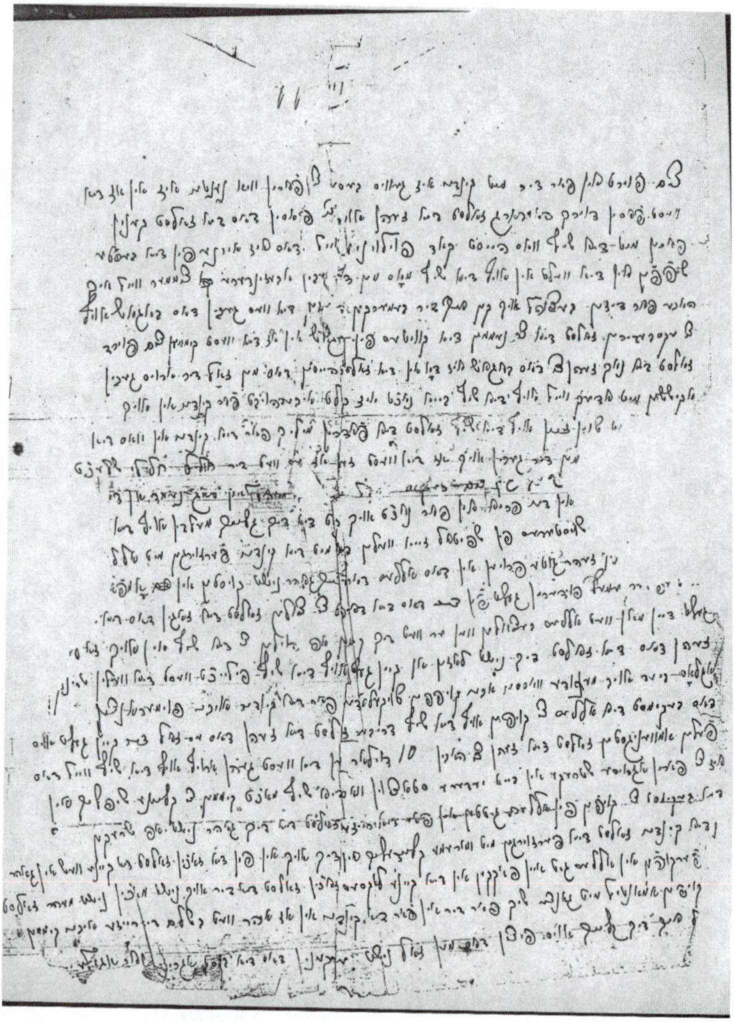

10. Raquel to Yaacov:

Warsaw, March 16, 1922.

Dear, beloved husband Yaacov:

I received at last your letter of January 25, the one I waited for, for such a long time and with so many hopes! But, when I read it, instead of receiving the happiness I so dreamed of, that would relieve the pain in my heart, I felt enormous pain! Such sorrow that a pen cannot describe. I thought that my eyes and my heart had no more tears left from crying so much. My darkest sorrow is that there is no place anywhere for me and my little sons—I am being pushed everyday from one place to another—I am being insulted, cursed.

But even before I had finished reading your letter, it was as if a new fountain opened and my tears ran and ran from my eyes like water, because of your sorrows, your pains! And I scream: What's happening? Pain and suffering within, mine and my children's; pain and suffering on account of your illness . . . When will all this end?

Tsarot Veiesurim. Yes. There are still miracles. Here we are in good health, thank God. But *lo kol yom mitrachech nissim*: miracles don't happen every day. My strengths weaken from so much sadness. Can the milk that nurses my little son continue to flow from a sour heart? Impossible! I was thinking that in a little while salvation might come! That we would be traveling towards you, my beloved, the consolation of my soul; that soon my tear-filled eyes would shine again, to see how the father will hold his sons to his chest and kiss them with all his might.

But in the end the salvation of a mother and her children move away further and we are bathed in a sea of loneliness and misery, of filth and mud. Do I have to bear how my sister goes about with a long face without saying a word to me? I have to put up with my brother-in-law shouting and insulting me and my sons and see how our older son David sits all day, pounding his mattress; and at night he's never allowed to run around the house, as a boy needs to do. Oh! How can one stand all this? My heart bursts! They say that one becomes accustomed to one's *tsarot*. But now your illness is a new *tsarah* for me. You write to me that you're going to see the doctor a second time, and you hope the third time he will let you leave the hospital? Oh! I hope that you're right. For the sake of our two little sons, may heaven restore their father's health! But my heart trembles with fear, thinking that you are only writing me of your recovery to make me feel better, but that in truth you are still sick. Otherwise, you would have hurried the papers to us, to save us from our misery. Forgive me, but these thoughts torment me.

You write me that your sister Helke—God keep her in good health for many years—is doing for you what not even a mother could do. From the depths of my heart I thank her for her devotion for you. God help her in everything that she is trying to do. I'd like to ask you, my dear husband, now that your sister is doing so much for you, that you speak with her and beg her on your knees, with tears, that she save your wife and little sons from this prison . . . that she takes us away from here. This would be a miracle for her too, as I am a living being and I could help to lighten her burden.

Dear husband, send your money in checks in Rifkele's name (Rifka Lipovich) to the following address: Geusha 72-43 for Rochze Liberman. Regarding the $5 dollars (52.80 German marks), I wrote to you a long time ago I had received them and how much they gave me for them.

I end my letter with the hope that you'll recover soon and that somehow you'll get us out of here so that we can always be together, and then all our hopes will come true. This will be our *Yeshuah.* (Salvation) Kisses and greetings from Raquel.

The children greet and kiss you. With God's help they will grow up in an easier way. I send sincere warm regards to my sister-in-law Helke Muller. I thank her hundreds of times for her efforts and the sacrifice she makes for you. At the same time I beg her to take pity on us and put an end to our *tsarot.*

Dear sister-in-law, please read the letter I wrote to my husband. Regards to you and to my brother-in-law Moshe Muller. May they live for many years.

Only my two little ones sustain me in my sufferings here. Maybe because of them, I will still be able to save myself. But the provider of our salvation, and help, has to be you. Only you, my dear husband, and no other, because a wife and a husband are a single person. Then, can you be satisfied when your own flesh and blood is struggling in suffering and pain, in cold, in tears and ice, in fights and offenses?

I wrote to you several times. I only ask you for the tickets for myself and the children, to my name, Ruchla Liberman. Write Rachel Liberman so I can finally breath without the terrible sorrows I live with.

And now, some news to console you, after all the news I wrote to you about, which were not the best. In answer to your qustion regarding the *mitzvot* that were performed in the *Brit mila (circumcision)*: The *Sandek* (who holds the baby in his arms) was Yudl Piascovsky. The godparents were her sister Rivka and her husband. The rest were townspeople: honest, religious people. Nu, we'll talk about all this *me pe le pe* (from mouth to mouth) when we are together.

Your wife greets you with her thoughts and very soon in person. Warm regards to my dear sister-in-law Helke Muller and my dear brother-in-law Moshe.

Dear Helke, I beg you very much to read the letter I wrote to my husband. I believe you will be the messenger of our salvation, and that just as you started the *mitzva* (the good did) you will continue to help us in our situation. You are the one who will help put an end to our suffering and help my children to get an education and be happy. With your husband and mine together, I hope you can take us away from here. Your sister-in-law greets you with warmth and with tears, Rochle Ferber.

Our children, Ioshuah David and Moshe Velvele send their greetings, Daddy. Moshe Velvele thanks you for the dollars you sent him. When you can give him money personally he will thank you and kiss you much more. Adieu.

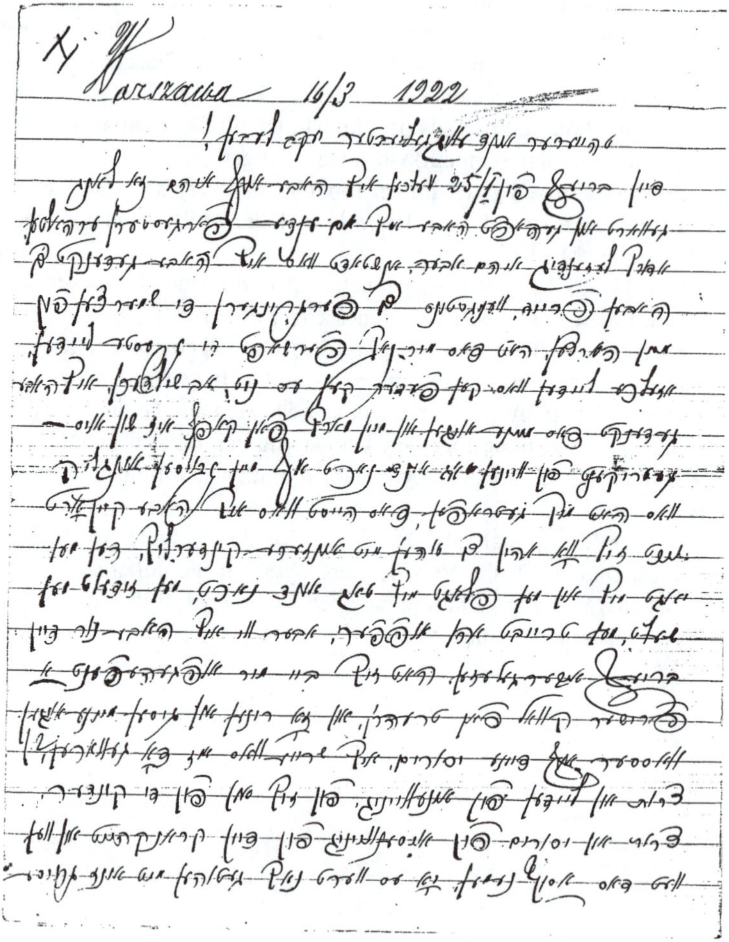
Warszawa 16/3 1922

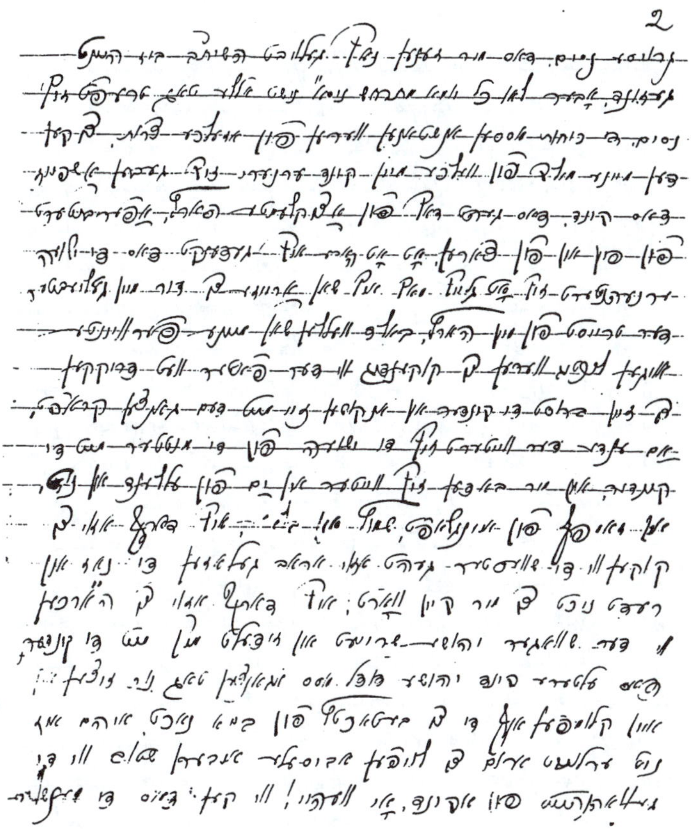

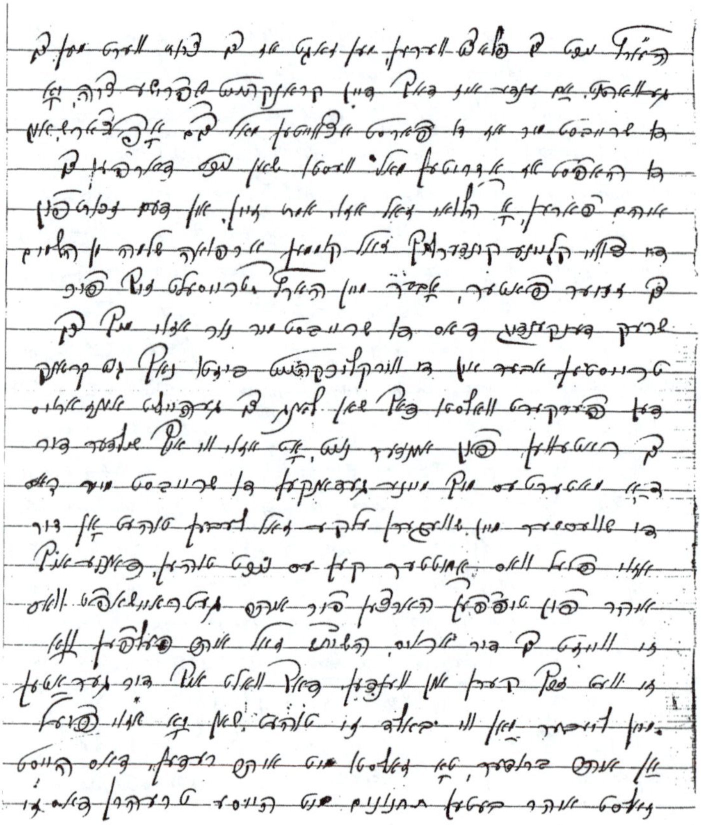

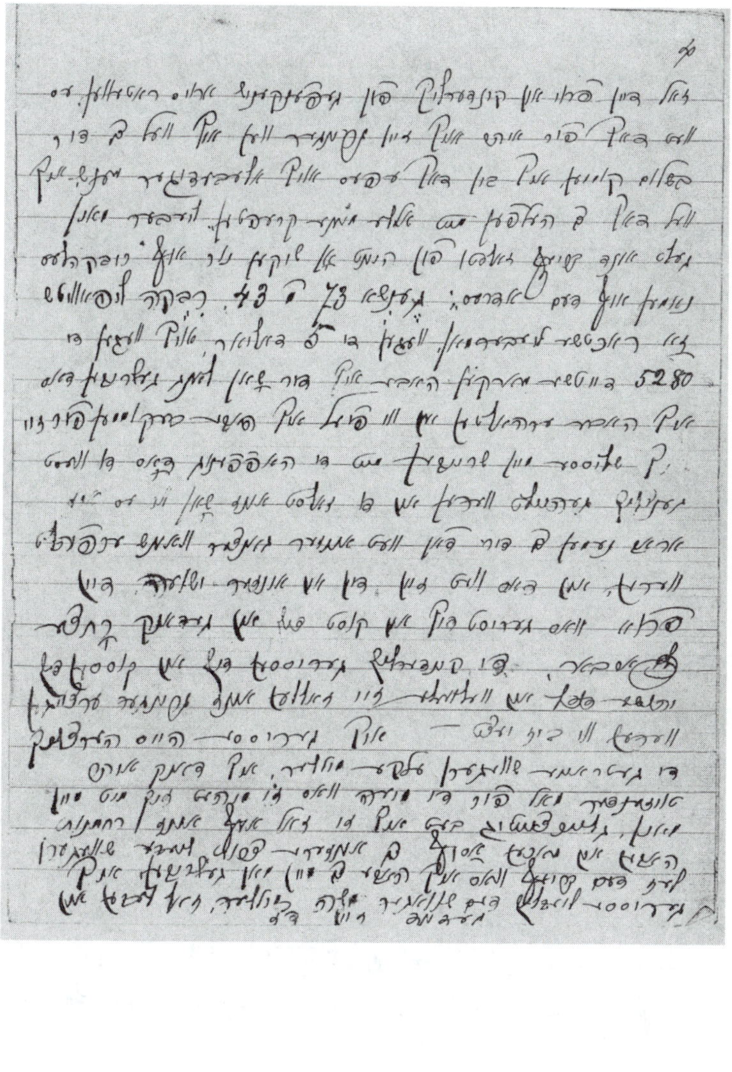

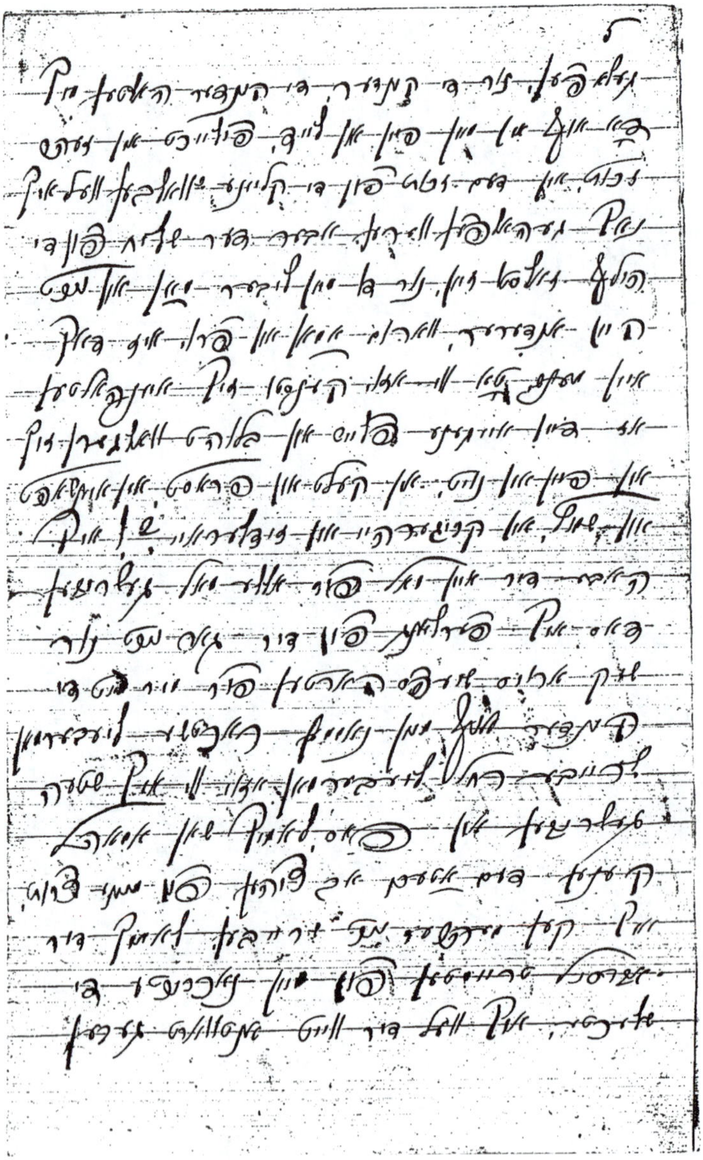

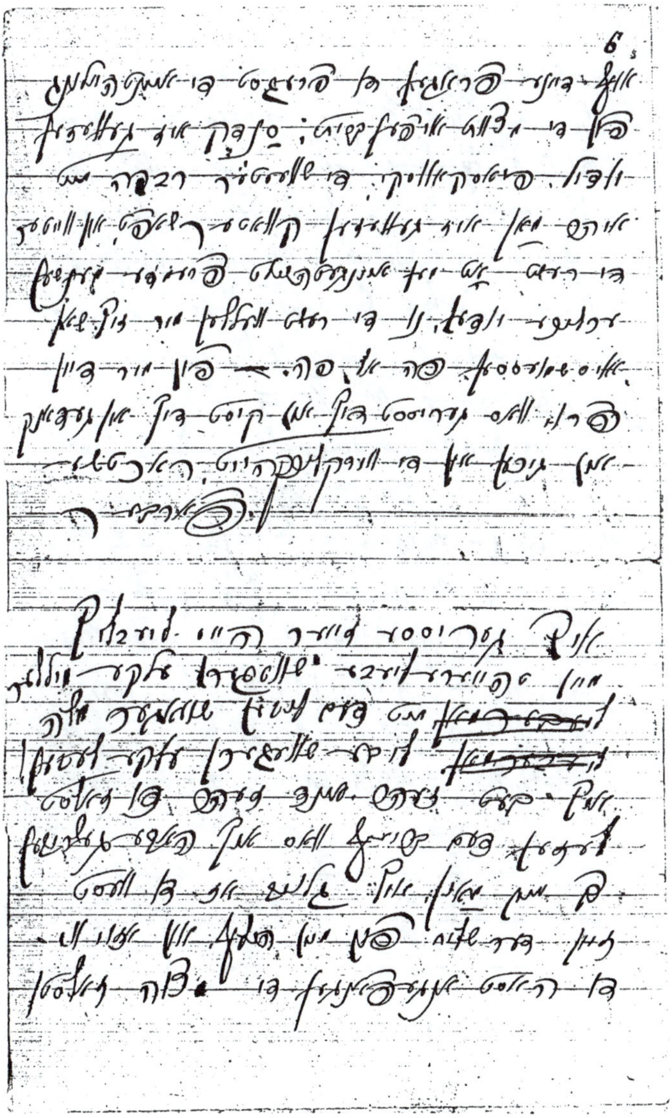

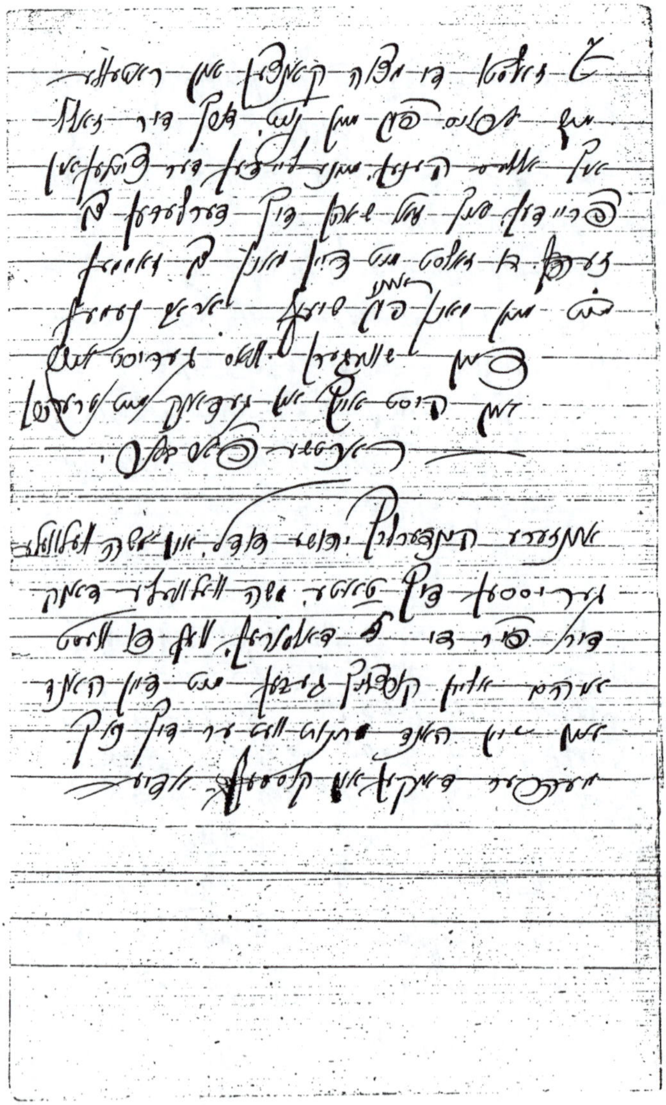

11. Raquel to Yaacov:

Warsaw, April 20, 1922 (last day of Passover).

My dear and faithful husband Yaacov:

I received your letter of March 16, 1922 yesterday. My happiness because soon our correspondence will be over and we'll see each other face to face, is boundless. We'll still have to wait a few more weeks for that to happen. My two lovely and adored children and I will be patient because we know what a splendid future brightens our eyes and renews our strength, to withstand everything else more easily. I see our salvation coming closer. Especially now, that my sister and brother-in-law's behavior towards me is better than before, when they thought they'd have to put up with us for a very long time, maybe for years. But now, seeing we are leaving, they show respect for me once again. Like the Jews, who were ill-treated and enslaved by the Egyptians, but thought of with respect after they left. It's the same with me. My oppressors also respect me now. We'll talk about it later on. Nu, as they say, *sof tov, hakol tov*: "All's well that ends well."

Now, my dear husband, regarding your question as to why I had written that you should send me the money and the tickets to the Rivkele's address, the reason was that I had thought that after Pessach I would be forced to move away from here, from my brother-in-law's Yoshua, to Rivkele's house. But now I see that I'll remain here until . . . in a *guter shu*, (happily) we board. So I ask you to send the money in Yoshuah's name, and also the tickets, but that you should write the name of Raquel Leah Liberman.

I received the 35.- dollars and I got for them 129,000 Polish marks. I give you the particulars again: In the passport I appear as Raquel Leah Liberman, and our little Moshe Velvele, appears as Mishka Wolf Liberman. Well, I believe all is clear now.

I'm writing on a separate sheet to my sister-in-law. You'll surely see her and will be able to read her my letter. Take very good care of yourself. May you keep in good health. These are the wishes of your faithful and dear wife, Ruchka Ferber.

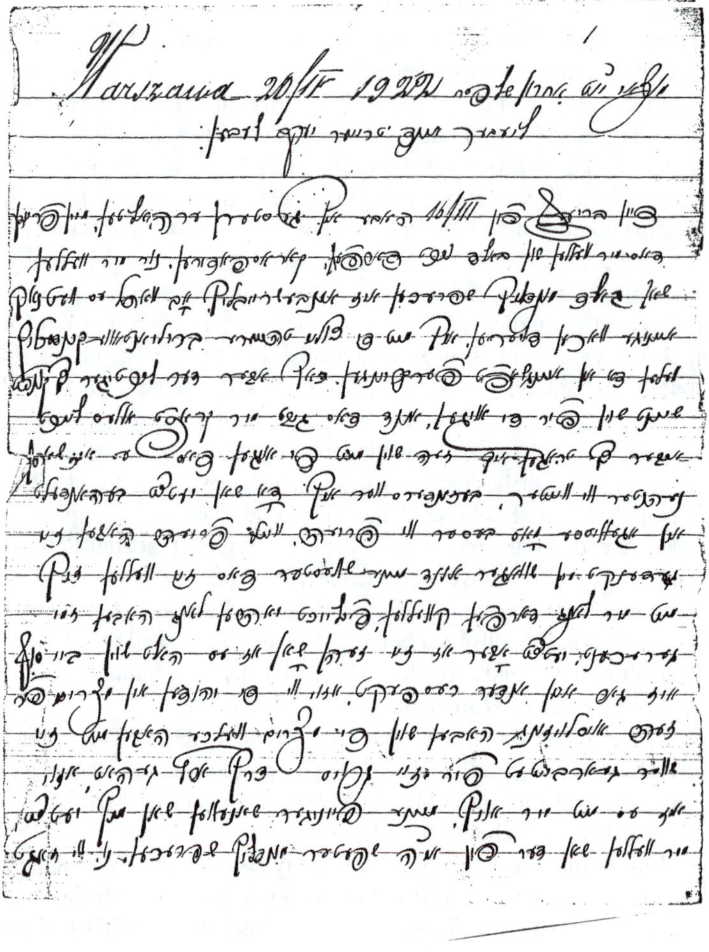
Warszawa 20/III 1922

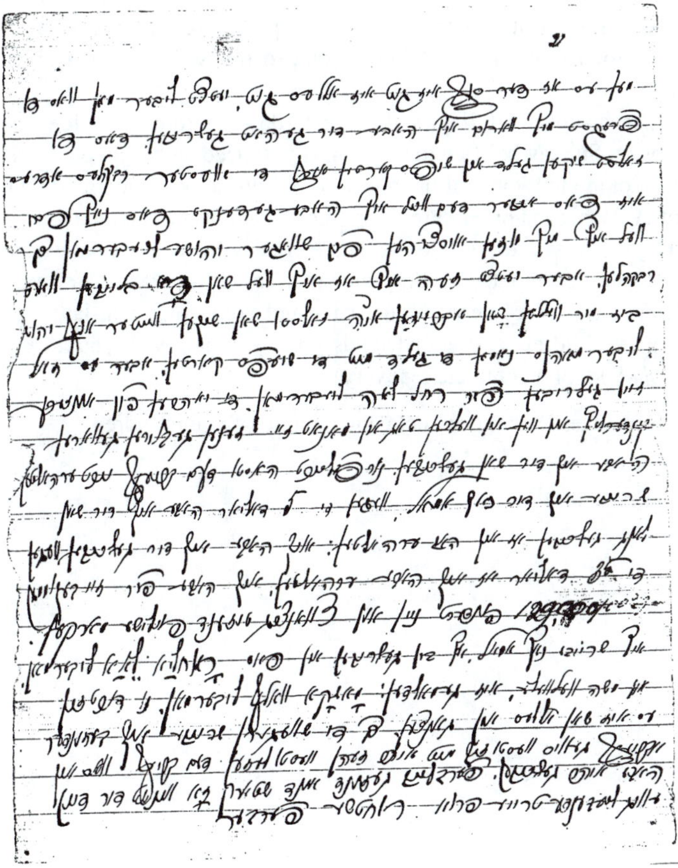

12. Helke to Her Brother Yaacov, in Hospital:

Tapalqué, July 27, 1923

Dear brother Yaacov:

I received your dear letter from the hospital. We were all standing up when Raquel read it. You can't imagine the emotions everyone felt when we received it, coming from the hospital! We all shouted in one voice: "Good God, help us! Put an end to our worries and and our anguish!"

Dear brother: I tell you that yesterday I wrote to Yalen, and perhaps on Sunday he'll go to see you. If you need anything, please tell Yalen. Let me tell you that the return to our house was good, and that I found everything in order here. Once more, dear brother, let me tell you it was good of you to write to us, since your wife couldn't believe me when I told her about you. So your letter served to wake us all up. I don't have any more news. Your sister and your brother-in-law; your wife, your children, and your friends greet you and wish you a quick *refua shelimah* (a complete recovery)

Your sister Helke. I'm enclosing a photo of your children.

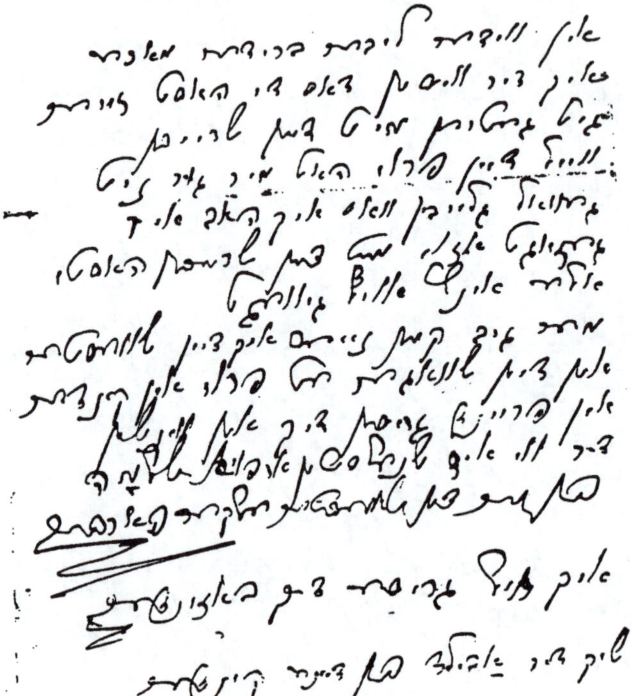

II. LETTERS TRANSLATED FROM SPANISH INTO ENGLISH:

1. Helke, Raquel's Sister-in-Law to Raquel:

Tapalqué July 12, 1925

Dear Sister-in-law:

Here I'm sending your your fortune. Don't get me mad. This is so you can see nothing is going wrong around here. And don't frighten me with telegrams. They lack nothing. They are dressed casually. This is just so you calm down.

Greetings from your sister-in-law
Elke

2. Eugenia, Raquel's Friend, to Raquel:

Buenos Aires, November 2, 1933.

Dear sister Rosita:

I hope that when you receive this letter you're enjoying good health. Your children and us, we are well. Dear Rosita: If I didn't write to you sooner, is because you know how busy I am. The children are also very busy with their homework.

You write to me in your last letter that if I don't write to you it means that I've taken offense. You know very well I don't have any reason to be offended and I beg you never to think that way.Your children are very well. They behave and study very well. Jacobo came on the 30th to Buenos Aires. I went to speak to Elena because Mauricio was not there. He said that on the first he would hand you over the business, so wait patiently, as it will be allright. Without any more news, a strong kiss from your little sister who wants to see you happy,

Eugenia Elisa

3. David, Raquel's Older Son, to His Mother:

Dear Mamita:

I would like to see you soon by my side, but since that is impossible, for the moment I live happily with your memory and with the knowledge that you love me, just as I love you.

Your son, David

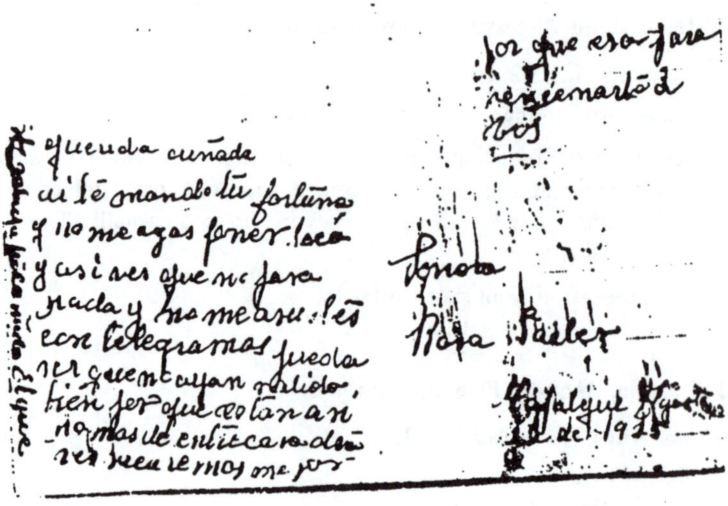

Bs. As. Marzo 2 – 1933

Querida hermanita Rosita

Que al recibo de ésta te encuentres gozando bien
de salud; nosotros y tus hijitos estamos bien.
Querida Rosita si yo no te contesté antes es porque tu
sabes lo ocupada que estoy y los chicos muy ocupados con sus
deberes.
Tú me escribes en la última carta que si yo no te escribo
es porque estoy sentida + bien sabes que yo no tengo porque
estarlo y te pido que no pienses nunca esto
Tus hijitos están lo más bien se portan y estudian lo más
lindo
Jacobo vino a Bs.As. el 30.
Y fui hablar con Clem porque Mauricio no estaba y me
que el 1° te iba ha entregar el negocio así que espera
tranquila que todo se arreglará

Sin más se despide con un fuerte beso
tu hermanita que quiere verte feliz

Eugenia y Elvira

Querida mamita desearia verte pronto a mi lado pero ya que esto es imposible por el momento viva con tu recuerdo feliz y el saber que tu me quieres lo mismo que yo

tu hijo

David

4. Mauricio, Raquel's Younger Son, to His Mother:

Dear Mamita:

David loves you no less than I do. And although I am little, my love for you is great.

Your son, Mauricio

5. Second note added in 1963 by son David on the reverse of his mother's portrait, taken in Poland in 1919:

Picture in homage to the most sublime person on earth:
THE MOTHER
Arrangement (fixture) made up by myself with lots of love.

Josué D. Ferber
11-1-1963

6. Note written in back of Raquel's photograph:

Picture with the photo of our dear mother, prepared on the eve of Wednesday, February 6, 1957, at 12:15 a.m.

With love,
Josué D. Ferber

Correction: It is already Thursday the 7th, 15 minutes after the new day.

Querida mamita: si D. aad. te quiere; no mira to que
chico
y aunque soy mu pariso sea muy hacia ti. tu hijo

Mauricio

Cuarteto en homenaje
a tu figura más sublime
de la tierra.

LA MADRE →

Arreglo hecho por mí
con todo cariño José V. Ferrer

11-1-1963
1963
11-1-63

17 (

11-1-63

Cuadrito con la foto de nuestra
querida madre, armado en la
noche del día 6-2-1957 "minutos"
siendo las 24 y 15 horas, con todo
Cariño

José D. Ferber

Aclaración: siendo el
día 7 y ... les
0,15 minutos del día
7 minutos

CHAPTER VI
Photographs

The first picture of Raquel Liberman was taken at a photographic studio in 1919 in Lodz. It portrays a fair skinned, romantic-looking girl, with a dreamy and perceptive gaze. She dresses formally, in black. Her hand rests on her long skirt, holding a rose. The openness of her dress, covered by dark lace, is adorned by a long necklace of white pearls.

The two inscriptions at the opposite side of her portrait were written by her older son, José Ferber, half a century later. The interval between the date of the photo—1919—and that of the inscription—1963—makes the discrepancy between the photo that José must have kept hidden for so many years, and the text that expresses his strong feelings for his mother significant: The inscription states:

This is a picture with the photo of our dear mother, prepared on the eve of the 6/2/57, Wednesday, at 8:15 p.m.

With great love, José Ferber.

There is a meticulous correction at one corner of the inscription that states:

Clarification: It is already Thursday, the 7th, at 7 a.m.

A second inscription of this beautiful photograph states:

"This is a picture that pays homage to the most sublime figure on earth: the mother. Fixture made by myself. "
With great love. José D. Ferber, 11-1-1963."

The photos in which Raquel is posing with her two sons, one at each side of her, are taken within one or two years intervals. They show the changes that took place as her children were growing up. Raquel is striking for her maternal, possessive appearance. Already freed from her captors and established in Buenos Aires with her sons, her face discloses a smile of contentment, even of triumph.

In contrast, the photos of Raquel that show a desolate landscape of grey background. In one of them Raquel is standing in a deserted alley, with an arm leaning against a lamp-post. In the other, she is standing alone in the street. In both of these pictures Raquel looks older, wrinkled. Her make-up weighs heavily against her face, like clay over porcelain. One could well ask what motive compelled this woman to leave such pathetic testimony of her unhappiness.

THE DRESS

The dressing is another important aspect of the photos. During the 1930s, when there were still no instantaneous photos nor the films with many negatives, one pose had to include all the details one wanted to show the public. That is why Raquel dresses so carefully in her photos with her children. She makes sure that both children wear exactly the same design of sailor suits, or that following the Basque fashion they wear a red sachet round their waist, black trousers, and long, white stockings. On these formal occasions, when one expects seriousness, Raquel cannot repress a smile of satisfaction.

It is to be observed that when Raquel receives pictures of her children from Tapalqué, a note in the back of one of the photos justifies their way of dressing. The note could have been been written by Raquel's sister-in-law, Helke, or perhaps by the woman who took care of her chidren, which explains that her purpose is only to remind their mother how much they love her. They excuse themselves for the unkempt appearance of their clothes, explaining that they are dressed plainly, in house clothes. The children implore Raquel,

"Dear mamita," her sons implore her: "don't cry so much".

PHOTOS OF RAQUEL LIBERMAN AND HER RELATIVES:

1. 1919. Portrait of Ruchla (Raquel) Liberman, age 19, Warsaw, Poland.
2. 1921. Yaacov Ferber, on board in Marseille, France, going to Argentina.
3. 1922. Raquel with her husband Yaacov and her sister-in-law Helke, in the port of Buenos Aires.
4. 1925. Raquel and her two sons, one of them standing on a chair.
5. 1925. Helke with her husband dressed as a gaucho, and their two nephews in Tapalqué, a village in the province of Buenos Aires.
6. 1925. Helke and the woman who looked after ther children in Tapalqué. One of the boys is sitting down.
7. 1925. Raquel bathing with her sister and brother-in-law in the salt lake of Epecuén, Carhué, Argentina.
8. 1926. Raquel sitting, with her two children in sailors suits.
9. 1927. Raquel standing alone in the street, wearing a fur coat.
10. 1928. Raquel, alone, leaning against a street lamp.
11. 1928. Raquel sitting, wearing a checkered dress.
12. 1930. Raquel, Helke and her older son Sruga Dudl (David).
13. 1931. Helke and her husband with Raquel's two boys.
14. 1933. Raquel with her sons, one of them wearing a school uniform.
15. Raquel with her sons, wearing a Spanish outfit.
16. Raquel, wearing a hat.
17. Raquel, wearing a black dress.
18. 1937. Raquel's two sons.

1. Portrait of Rochla (Raquel Liberman, age 19, Warsaw, Poland.

2. Yaacov Ferber, on board in Marielle, France, going to Argentina.

3. Raquel with her husband Yaacov and her sister-in-law Helke, in the port of Buenos Aires.

with her husband dressed as a gaucho, and their two nephews
ué, a village in the province of Buenos Aires.

4. Raquel and her two sons, one

5. Helke
in Tapalq

6. Helke and the woman who looked after ther children in Tapalqué.
One of the boys is sitting down.

7. Raquel bathing with her sister and brother-in-law in the salt lake of
Epecuén, Carhué, Argentina.

8. Raquel sitting, with her two children in sailors suits.

9. Raquel standing alone in the street, wearing a fur coat.

10. Raquel, alone, leaning against a street lamp.

11. Raquel sitting, wearing a checkered dress.

12. Raquel, Helke and her older son Sruga Dudl (David).

13. Helke and her husband with Raquel's two boys.

14. Raquel with her sons, one of them wearing a school uniform.

15. Raquel with her sons, wearing a Spanish outfit.

16. Raquel, wearing a hat.

17. Raquel, wearing a black dress.

18. Raquel's two sons.

PHOTOGRAPHS AND DOCUMENTATION OF THE ZWI MIGDAL:

1. Luis Migdal, founder of the *Zwi Migdal* Organization. Newspaper photo and tombstone.
2. The main site of the *Zwi Migdal* organization, from where the main activities were organized.
3. Entrance to the "ruffian" cemetery which shows the same gate as the main Jewish cemetery in Villa Domínico, Buenos Aires.
4. Partial views of the Jewish cemetery.
5. Excerpt from the newspaper *Crítica*, revealing the verdict against those involved in the white slave trade, Sept. 30, 1930.

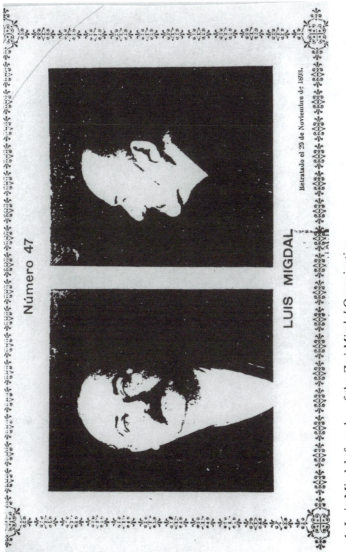

1. Luis Migdal, founder of the *Zwi Migdal* Organization.

2. The main site of the *Zwi Migdal* organization, from which the main
activities were organized.

3. Entrance to the "ruffian" cemetery, which shows the same gate as that of the main Jewish cementary in Villa Domínico, Buenos Aires.

4.Partial views of the Jewish cemetery

4. *(continued)*

5. Excerpt from the newspaper Critica, revealing the verdict against those involved in the white slave trade, Sept. 30, 1930

Bibliography

Aleichem, Sholem, (Pseudonym of Solomon Rabinovich), "The man from Buenos Aires," *Tevye's Daughters*. New York, Crown Publications, 1945.

Alpersohn, Marcos. *Dreissig Jahren in Argentina* Vol 1,(Berlin, 1923) Ch. 2.

Alsogaray, Julio, *Trilogía de la trata de blancas: Rufianes-policía-municipalidad*. Buenos Aires, Editorial Tor, 1933.

Arlt, Roberto. "Que no queden aguas de borrajas," *Diario El Mundo*," Buenos Aires, April 6, 1930.

Asch, Shalom. *God of Vengeance*. Boston, 1918 ed.

Asch, Shalom. *Mottke The Thief*, New York, E.P. Putnam and Sons, 1935.

Béter, Clara. (pseudonym of César Tiempo). *Verses of a. . .* Buenos Aires, Editorial Rescate, 1926.

Botoshansky, Jacobo. "Algunos recuerdos sobre *Ibergus*," Buenos Aires, Centro de Artistas Judíos, 28-6-1926.

Botoshansky, Jacob. "Some memories about *Ibergus*:To Leib Malach, in memoriam, a year after his death in 1936", *Di Presse*, 1936.

Bra, Gerardo. *La organización negra: La increíble historia de la Zwi Migdal*, Buenos Aires, Ediciones Corregidor, 1982.

Bristow, Edward. *Prostitution and Prejudice: The Jewish Fights Against White Slavery*, London, Oxford University Press, 1982.

Casadevall, Domingo F. *El tema de la mala vida en el teatro nacional*. Buenos Aires, Editorial Kraft, 1927.

Chas de Cruz, Israel. *Aventuras de la picaresca porteña*, Buenos Aires, Editorial Freeland, 1966, 17-21.

Costantini, Humberto. *Rapsodia de Raquel Liberman*, in *Cien años de narrativa judeo-argentina*, Milá, Buenos Aires 1989, 194- 202.

Drumont, Edouard. *La France Juive*, Paris, Margon & Flammarion, 1885.

Eichelbaum, Samuel. *Nadie la conoció nunca*. Buenos Aires: Centro Editor de América Latina, 1968 (Written in 1926).

Eichelbaum, Samuel. *Nadie la conoció nunca* (Buenos Aires, Ediciones del Carro de Tespis, 1956).

Gálvez, Manuel. *Nacha Regules*, Buenos Aires, Centro Editor de América Latina, 1968.

Glickman, Nora *Modern Jewish Studies*, New York, Queens College Publications, 1989, 17-32.

Glickman, Nora. "The Jewish White Slave Trade in Latin American Writings," *American Jewish Archives:New Perspectives on Latin American Jewry*, Ed. Judith Laikin Elkin, xxxiv, 2, Nov. 1982.

Glickman, Nora Ed. *Una tal Raquel*, unedited version.

Goldar, Ernesto. *La mala vida*, Buenos Aires, Centro Editor de América Latina, 1971, p. 48.

Guy, Donna. *Sex and Danger in Buenos Aires*. Lincoln: University of Nebraska Press, 1991.

Kordon, Bernardo. *El Mundo Israelita*, December 22, 1985. J.A. Report (1936) 34. Laikin Elkin, Judith, Nov. 1982, 178- 189.

Londres, Albert. *The Road to Buenos Ayres*, Blue Ribbon Books, New York, 1928. Translated by Eric Sutton as *The Road to Buenos Ayres* London: Constable, 1928.

Londres, Albert. *El camino de Buenos Aires* (Buenos Aires, Aga Taura, 1927), p. 7.

Londres, Albert. *The Road to Buenos Ayres* New York, 1928. *Argentiner YWO Shriftn*, Buenos Aires, 1955.

Malach, Leib. *Don Domingo's Crossroads* Ed. B. Kletzkin, Editorial Vilna, Poland, 1930; and E.L. Peretz Publishing House, Israel.

Malach, Leib. *Regeneración*. Translation of Leib Malach's play *Ibergus* from the Yiddish into Spanish by Rosalía Rosembuj and Nora Glickman. Preliminary study by Nora Glickman, "La trata de blancas." Buenos Aires: Editorial Pardés, 1984.

Malach, Leib. "Letter from Abroad: Two generations in the Argentine," *The Menorah Journal*, XIII, 1927, 408-416.

Malach, Lotty, Ed. *Leib Malach, vida y obra*. Comité del Libro "Leib Malach", Los Angeles: 1949.

Martel, Julián. *La bolsa*, Buenos Aires, Editorial Huemul, S.A., 1957.

Mirelman, Víctor. *En búsqueda de una identidad*, Buenos Aires, Editorial Milá, 1988.

Muñoz, Alicia. *Las crónicas de Pichincha*, Buenos Aires, n.d.

Novión, Alberto. *El cambalache de Petroff*, Revista Teatral *Nuestro Teatro*, Buenos Aires, April 1937.

Onega, Gladys. *La inmigración en la literatura Argentina: 1800-1910* Santa Fé, 1965, p. 132.

Ravitch, Melech. "Jewish Criticism on Leib Malach: *Don Domingo's Crossroads*: A Novel of Great Reach," in *Leib Malach: Work and Life* Ed. Lotty F. Malach, Los Angeles, 1949.

Senkman, Leonardo. *La identidad judía en la literatura argentina*. Buenos Aires: Pardés, 1983.

Scliar, Moacyr. *O ciclo das águas*, Porto Alegre, Editora Globo, 1978.

Scliar, Moacyr. "Nas sombras do passado," *Shalom*. Rio de Janeiro, June 1993, 3-5.

Serrano, Carlos Luis. *Teatro: Raquel Liberman, una historia de Pichincha*. Rosario, Editorial Ross, 1992.

Shalom, Myrta. "Te llamarás Raquel," unedited, presented in Buenos Aires television, 1993.

Sholem Aleichem, (Pseudonym of Solomon Rabinovich), "The man from Buenos Aires," *Tevye's Daughters* New York, Crown Publications, 1945.

Singer, Isaac B., "The Colony," *A Friend of Kafka and Other Stories* New York, Farrar, Strauss & Giroux, 1970.

Singer, Isaac, "Hanka," *Passions* (Grenwich:Fawcet Books, 1915).

Szichman, Mario. *A las 20:25 la señora entró en la inmortalidad*, Hanover, Ediciones del Norte, 1981.

Viñas, David. *En la Semana Trágica* Buenos Aires, José Alvares, 1966.

Viñas, David. *Los dueños de la tierra* Buenos Aires, Editorial Librería Lorraine, 1974.

Weisbrot, Robert. *The Jews of Argentina* Philadelphia, Jewish Publication Society, 1979.

Index

Aleichem, Scholem, 17, 19, 20, 190n
Alpersohn, Marcos, 15n, 188n
Alsogaray, Julio, x, 13, 14, 16, 63,
    64n, 188n
Appelfeld, Aaron, 49, 60, 64n
Arlt, Roberto, 8, 16n, 188n
Asch, Shalom, 17, 49n, 188n

Bardevere, Enzo, 43
Bassero, Victorio Luis, 16n
Béter, Clara, (see also Tiempo,
    César) 34-37, 50n, 188n
Botoshansky, Jacobo, 49n, 188n
Bra, Gerardo, 8, 16n, 188n
Bristow, Edward, 7, 13, 15n, 16n,
    64n, 188n

Casadevall, Domingo, 188n
Castelnuovo, Elías, 50n
Catán-Petorossi, Marambio, 29
Cavanesi, Iriarte, 29
Chas de Cruz, Israel, 40, 51n, 188n
Contoursi-Terés, 29
Costantini, Humberto, 62, 64n, 188n

Demme, Jonathan, 41, 48, 53
De la Torre, Lisandro, 42, 43
Drumont, Edouard, 4, 15n, 188n

Echeverría, Esteban, 47
Eichelbaum, Samuel, 31, 32, 50n,
    189n
Ezrat Nashim, 8, 14, 55, 56

Ferber, Yaacov, x, 56, (Chapter IV,
    Documentation: 82-91; Ch V,
    Correspondence: Letters translated
    from the Yiddish: 95-149; 84-91,
    Letters translated from the
    Spanish, 149-157.
Feijó, Bedia, 43

Gálvez, Manuel, 30, 31, 50n, 189n
Glickman, Nora, 15n, 20, 63, 64n,
    189n
Goldar, Ernesto, 15n, 64n, 189n
Guiraldes, Ricardo, 36
Guy, Donna, 14, 15n, 16n, 30, 50n,
    189n

Hirsch, Maurice de, 4

Irizarry, Esther, 35, 36

Jusid, Juan, 42

Kordon, Bernardo, 4, 15n, 189n

Lambertucci, Roldán, 29
Liberman, Raquel, x, xi, Chapter III,
    Historical Version: 51-53, The
    unkonwn Raquel: 53-60; Raquel in
    fiction, 60-63; Chapter IV,
    Documentation: 63-82; Ch V,
    Correspondence: Letters translated
    from Yiddish, 93-150; letters trans-
    lated from Spanish, 151-155;
    Chapter VI, Photographs, 157-158.
Lincovsky, Cipe, 45, 46
Londres, Albert 3, 10, 11, 16n, 40,
    44, 189n

Malach, Leib, 8, 15n, 20-26, 49n, 63,
    189n
Malach, Lotty, 189n
Martel, Julián, (see also Miró, Juan
    María) 29, 50n, 189n
Martínez Estrada, Ezequiel, 45, 46,
    51n
Migdal, Luis, 181
Mirelman Victor, 8, 15n, 189n
Miró, Juan María, 29
Muñoz, Alicia, 33, 50n, 189n

Novión, Alberto, 28, 29, 50n, 190n

Onega, Gladys, 4, 15n, 190n

polaca, polacas, ix, 7, 10, 22, 26, 27,
    30, 38, 39, 40, 42, 43, 45, 46, 63
Pareja, Ernesto, 15, 16n, 38-40, 42,
    43, 45

Rosas, Juan Manuel de, 47
Ravitch, Melech, 50n, 190n
Rodriguez Ocampo, Manuel, 13, 55,
    58, 59, 63

Roldán-Lambertucci, 29
Rosembuj Rosalía, x, 15n, 20, 64n

Sarmiento, Domingo Faustino, 4
Scliar, Moacyr, 38, 51n, 190n
Senkman, Leonardo, 36, 50n, 190n
Serrano, Carlos Luis, 53, 54, 62, 63,
    64n, 190n
Shalom, Myrta, 62, 63, 64n, 190n
Sheider, Roy, 48
Shrader, Leonard, 45
shtetl, 19, 37, 40, 44, 62, 93
Sholem Aleichem, 190n
Singer, Isaac B., 26-28, 50n, 190n
Stagnaro, Juan Bautista, 43
Szichman, Mario, 38, 51n, 190n

Tagini-Mutarelli, 29
Teigh Bloom, Murray, 48
Tiempo, César, 34-37, 50n, 188n

Uriburu, José F., 14, 43

Valentino, Rudolf, 45
Viñas, David, 31, 33, 50n, 190n
Visca, Cadícamo, 29

Weisbrot, Robert, 14, 16n, 190n
white slave trade, ix x, 3-17 (in
    Yiddish fiction, 17-28; in Latin
    American fiction, 28-41; in cine-
    ma, 41-49)

Yrigoyen, Hipólito, 14

Zwi Migdal ix, x, xi, 7, 8, 29, 30,
    40, 44-48, 55-60, 62, 63 (photo-
    graphs and documentation), 181-
    188